Editor-in-Chief and Founder:
  Lyndon H. LaRouche, Jr.
Editorial Board: *Lyndon H. LaRouche, Jr. , Helga
  Zepp-LaRouche, Robert Ingraham, Tony
  Papert, Gerald Rose, Dennis Small, Jeffrey
  Steinberg, William Wertz*
Co-Editors: *Robert Ingraham, Tony Papert*
Managing Editor: *Nancy Spannaus*
Technology: *Marsha Freeman*
Books: *Katherine Notley*
Ebooks: *Richard Burden*
Graphics: *Alan Yue*
Photos: *Stuart Lewis*
Circulation Manager: *Stanley Ezrol*

INTELLIGENCE DIRECTORS
Counterintelligence: *Jeffrey Steinberg, Michele
  Steinberg*
Economics: *John Hoefle, Marcia Merry Baker,
  Paul Gallagher*
History: *Anton Chaitkin*
Ibero-America: *Dennis Small*
Russia and Eastern Europe: *Rachel Douglas*
United States: *Debra Freeman*

INTERNATIONAL BUREAUS
Bogotá: *Miriam Redondo*
Berlin: *Rainer Apel*
Copenhagen: *Tom Gillesberg*
Houston: *Harley Schlanger*
Lima: *Sara Madueño*
Melbourne: *Robert Barwick*
Mexico City: *Gerardo Castilleja Chávez*
New Delhi: *Ramtanu Maitra*
Paris: *Christine Bierre*
Stockholm: *Ulf Sandmark*
United Nations, N.Y.C.: *Leni Rubinstein*
Washington, D.C.: *William Jones*
Wiesbaden: *Göran Haglund*

ON THE WEB
e-mail: eirns@larouchepub.com
www.larouchepub.com
www.executiveintelligencereview.com
www.larouchepub.com/eiw
Webmaster: *John Sigerson*
Assistant Webmaster: *George Hollis*
Editor, Arabic-language edition: *Hussein Askary*

EIR (ISSN 0273-6314) *is published weekly
(50 issues), by EIR News Service, Inc.,
P.O. Box 17390, Washington, D.C. 20041-0390.
(703) 297-8434*

European Headquarters: E.I.R. GmbH, Postfach
Bahnstrasse 9a, D-65205, Wiesbaden, Germany
Tel: 49-611-73650
Homepage: http://www.eir.de
e-mail: info@eir.de
Director: Georg Neudecker

Montreal, Canada: 514-461-1557
eir@eircanada.ca

Denmark: EIR - Danmark, Sankt Knuds Vej 11,
basement left, DK-1903 Frederiksberg, Denmark.
Tel.: +45 35 43 60 40, Fax: +45 35 43 87 57. e-mail:
eirdk@hotmail.com.

Mexico City: EIR, Sor Juana Inés de la Cruz 242-2
Col. Agricultura C.P. 11360
Delegación M. Hidalgo, México D.F.
Tel. (5525) 5318-2301
eirmexico@gmail.com

After the Summit: The Great Projects

Time to Break Ground

by Diane Sare, Manhattan

July 8—In the last few weeks, LaRouche PAC organizers have intersected a "mass-strike" phenomenon at campaign tables all over the country. The lead sign is "Defend Trump, Stop *Here,*" flanked by signs on China's Belt and Road Initiative, and pictures of Trump, Xi, and Putin wearing photo-shopped "Make America Great Again" hats. Organizers report that the rate of people pulling over and signing up is reminiscent of the summer of 2009, when Americans were up in arms about the impending murderous Obamacare.

Who are these people lining up to defend the President? They are patriotic Americans, formerly the working "middle class" of the United States, who were driven to desperation by the 60-year-old "post-industrial society" policy capped by the Bush-Obama looting scheme known as the "bailout." They are what both FDR and President Trump have called "the forgotten man."

At post offices in Long Island, Staten Island, New Jersey, and even in Manhattan, the people signing up are welders, bricklayers, pipefitters, carpenters, heating and air-conditioning techs, corrections officers, medical staff, and other working, or skilled and looking-for-work people. Many of their immediate family members have been casualties of the suicidal drug culture—although not all of them are willing to discuss it. They are mobilized, because after the defeat of the pro-Wall Street and pro-war-with-Russia Hillary Clinton, Obama's clone, in November, these forgotten men and women began to develop confidence in the power of their own voices. With the defeat of Hillary Clinton, they had finally made themselves heard.

Even as President Trump succeeds in wresting his foreign policy from the desperate grasp of the British

EDITORIAL

Imperial neocons—with important and successful meetings with President Putin and President Xi, as at the Hamburg G-20 gathering—the new relationship with these powerful nations gives him a greater potential to act within the United States to alleviate the desperate conditions currently faced by most Americans. It is urgent that Lyndon LaRouche's *Four Laws,* starting with the reinstatement of Glass-Steagall, and concluding with the fusion energy-driven platform, be taken up immediately.

First of all, the real physical infrastructure of the United States is crumbling. This is true across the whole nation, but is about to become the most obvious in New York City when the "Summer of Hell" begins this Monday, July 10, as 3 to 5 of Penn Station's 21 tracks are taken out of commission for badly needed repairs. Since March of this year, there have already been three derailments at Penn Station.

However, it is not only at Penn Station that the transportation infrastructure is in decrepit condition—there have been other derailments in the New York Metropolitan Transit Authority system, and the condition of the area's roads and bridges is no better. There is simply no room for shifting commuter traffic from one approach to another, and New York City is the place of employment for millions of people, so the outcry, if chaos sets in, will be heard around the world.

Of course, it's not just New York. Remember the February 2017 failure of the Oroville Dam spillway [see page 30], which threatened tens of thousands of Californians with being wiped out by a raging flood of water moving downhill, had the heavy rainstorms continued just a little longer.

That spillway is currently undergoing rapid reconstruction, demonstrating what is possible—but most people were unaware, prior to February, that the spillway had such serious flaws. How many other dams and levees are near breakpoint? Unpredictable and failing infrastructure can cost billions of dollars, not to mention many lives as well. There are a number of very fragile, crucial points of connection, such as the Soo Locks connecting Lake Superior and Lake Huron, or the Portal Bridge over the Hackensack River, which if they were to fail, would devastate the American economy, and which are badly in need of renovation or replacement.

The other, more pressing reason to act at once—that there is no time to waste on breaking ground—is that, as we saw in the elections last November, the American people have reached a breaking point. They are tired; they have been devastated by grief as their talented children die of opioid overdoses, or straight-out suicide. Our veterans are killing themselves in record numbers after returning from senseless wars only to lose their homes, or be denied medical care that they desperately need.

The fact that these people now have a President who actually cares about them, and loves the United States, has given them courage to hope that the future can be different from the past. This trust that the American people place in the current President is not to be taken lightly. If action is taken now, to curb the evil intent of Wall Street with Glass-Steagall, and to embrace the Chinese invitation to join the Belt and Road Initiative, as a pathway to implementation of the Four Laws of Lyndon LaRouche—if ground is immediately broken on a series of future-oriented, and desperately needed great projects—then this hope and optimism will surge forth, like a mighty chorus, accomplishing what was considered impossible only moments before. The American people are prepared for such action—now!

Most Positive Outcome of the G-20 Summit: The Putin-Trump Meeting

by Helga Zepp-LaRouche, chairwoman of the German political party,
Civil Rights Movement Solidarity (BüSo)

July 8—The presidents of the world's two greatest nuclear powers, U.S. President Donald Trump and Russian President Vladimir Putin, had their first face-to-face discussion on the sidelines of the Hamburg G-20 Summit, and according to U.S. Secretary of State Rex Tillerson, they established "a positive chemistry." Both Tillerson and Russian Foreign Minister Sergey Lavrov stressed that the discussion was constructive. And Trump said, "We look forward to a lot of very positive things happening for Russia, the United States, and everybody concerned."

Concretely, the two decided on a ceasefire in Syria and a new channel of communications on Ukraine. North Korea, terrorism, cyber-security, and new ambassadors were also discussed, among other things. Who, among those who are committed to world peace, could not be deeply relieved by such an outcome, which obviously must be followed up with further cooperation. Only the hardcore warmongers and over-zealous editors, like those at the *Washington Post*, were unable to hide their rage that the two foxes—and this I say with due respect—have outfoxed the trans-Atlantic neoliberal establishment. Because it was precisely to prevent this kind of U.S.-Russian cooperation—which Trump had promised during the election campaign—that the British as well as the American intelligence agencies, still staffed by appointees of the Obama Administration era, rigged the whole "Russia-gate" fairytale.

Merkel's Window-Dressing Smashed

Apart from this outstanding meeting, the Hamburg G-20 Summit demonstrated anew that the fragility of the old economic model of neoliberal globalization cannot be covered over with an attractive window dis-

kremlin.ru

U.S. President Donald Trump and Russian President Vladimir Putin.

play. Chancellor Merkel had obviously thought that Hamburg could present such a window-dressing, as the "Gateway to the World" and a symbol of global free trade.

And what came of this? An outlay of $130 million euros for an event during which the sherpas—due to the lack of substantial agreement among G-20 heads of state—had to haggle up to the last minute about the formulation of a final communiqué, in which the theme of climate change was essentially omitted. There was no discussion about, much less a solution for, the global financial system, whose glaring injustice increasingly widens the chasm between the poor and the rich—a situation against which the peaceful portion of demonstrators were there to protest, and which can lead to a crisis much worse than that of 2008 at any moment.

We now have to pay several million euros for the damage that the masked rioters caused—burned autos, broken windows, looted stores—not to mention the cost of medical treatment for more than 230 wounded policemen and an unknown number of others. How could the security situation have been so catastrophically misjudged? Interior Minister de Maizière had grandly declared before the summit that any violence would be nipped in the bud. We have just witnessed what that meant.

In May, the Interior Minister of Hamburg, Andy Grote, had announced quite arrogantly: "This is the opportunity to show heads of state with an autocratic, populist background how a vibrant democratic society functions, no matter how intense the confrontations are." He went on to say that "In principle this is a festival of democracy," and added that "The G-20 Summit will also be a showcase of modern police work." Federal government spokesman Steffen Seibert had declared in June 2016 that the Hamburg site fulfilled all the "logistical and technical security requirements" for the G-20 meeting.

The Hamburg chairman of the German police union, Jan Reinecke, blamed the politicians for the many wounded policemen and the destruction in the city: "Hamburg never should have been the venue for the G-20 Summit." In that he was right. What obviously was conceived as a shining stage production for Merkel's international diplomacy—wishful thinking that prevented a competent evaluation of the security situation—totally misfired.

The question naturally arises as to how such a blatant misevaluation of the potential for violence by a section of the demonstrators was possible. Given the total surveillance of the world's population by the NSA, GCHQ, and their various cooperation agreements with Germany's BND and other European intelligence services, it is astounding that the political class could have been so unaware of the danger. Equally disconcerting is the argument of the previously quoted Interior Minister of Hamburg, Andy Grote, that the police had not intervened when the hooligans rampaged in Hamburg's Schanzen District, because there was danger to "life and limb of the policemen." If the state can no longer protect the safety of its citizens, it has lost its monopoly on the use of force.

A Workable Model of Cooperation

Therefore what happened at this G-20 Summit should provide everyone the occasion to reflect on the premises of the current policy. Can a body like the G-20 ever come up with solutions to the existential challenges facing this world, if the sherpas, instead of agreeing on principles, fiddle around with formulas to paper over the differences? The G-20, founded in 1999, had already proved during the systemic crisis of 2008 that it was incapable of seizing the moment for the real reorganization of the bankrupt financial system. Instead, at the G-20 Summit in Washington on Nov. 15, 2008, the group set the course for the policy of quantitative easing with all its injustice, which led to the global revolts against this policy—from Brexit, to the election victory for President Trump, the "no" in the Italian referendum on constitutional changes, and even the peaceful part of the protest against the G-20 Summit in Hamburg.

A totally different model of cooperation between countries was recently demonstrated at the Silk Road Summit, at the Belt and Road Forum, in May in Beijing. There, 110 nations participated in a conference which was premised on "win-win" mutual cooperation for building the New Silk Road. This initiative has many aspects, such as the upgrading of international infrastructure, the development of industry and agriculture, cooperation in scientific research, cultural exchange, and cooperation on space exploration and research—to name only the most important areas.

Since this model of cooperation is based on real

principles, which take into account mutual interests and establish overall a higher level of reason, it functions in a harmonious way. Fortunately, it is gaining ground.

In addition to the summit between Trump and Putin, a broader, potentially very positive development emerged during the G-20 Summit. The recent worsening of the refugee crisis—in addition to the positive effect of the enormous Chinese investment in African railroads, dams, power plants, industrial parks, and agriculture—has apparently led Mrs. Merkel to realize that Germany must change its policy toward Africa. Shortly before the Hamburg Summit, all of her ministers were instructed to work out new concepts for trade and economic relations with Africa.

Then, during the meeting between President Xi and Chancellor Merkel, it was announced that China and Germany would jointly build a hydro-electric complex in Angola, which Merkel characterized as a model for further such cooperation. At the same time, there was a meeting in Berlin involving several ministries, at which the intensification of joint investment by Germany and China in Africa was discussed. That this was the first step in the right direction was obvious from the fact that the British *Economist* magazine found it necessary to attack Merkel's new Africa policy and to stress that she is by no means the new "leader of the free West."

Otherwise, the hysterical commentary in the *Washington Post* on the Trump-Putin summit not only makes it clear that their meeting was successful, but also that the mainstream media are the true enemies of mankind.

Thus, even though the G-20 summit was a disaster, everything is not so bad. The opportunities are definitely there to realize what the G-20 summit neglected to put on the agenda: The reorganization of the transAtlantic financial system through the enactment of the Glass-Steagall law, and the creation of a new credit system in the tradition of Alexander Hamilton, as well as collaboration by the United States and the European nations with the New Silk Road—above all, in economic development of Southwest Asia and Africa.

EIRContents

www.larouchepub.com Volume 44, Number 28, July 14, 2017

Bundesregierung/Kugler

Cover This Week

U.S. President Donald Trump and Russia President Vladimir Putin meet before the start of the retreat at the G-20.

Beautiful City

Όμορφη πόλη

by Dean Andromidas

PART III of Three Parts

The City and the Building of a Temple to the Republic

February 2017—A city is no city unless it honors its heroes, martyrs, and citizens who have made noble contributions to the city and country. A true memorial should commemorate the deeds of the past to instruct and inspire future generations. It must also express beauty. The ancient Hellenes always commemorated those who fell in battle to save their nation, especially those who died defending all of Greece from the two invasions of the Babylonian-Persian Empire. The building of the Parthenon was motivated not only by the need to rebuild the temples destroyed by the Persians, but also to celebrate the Greek victory with a living memorial.

As New York City entered the "postbellum" era, it experienced an explosion of economic development and expansion in all directions. Manhattan and eastern Brooklyn expanded beyond recognition as the Manhattan "grid" was filled up, and a new grid was laid out in Brooklyn. By the end of the second half of the 19th Century, the so-called "City Beautiful" movement came into being. It was promoted by a group of architects and sculptors, many of whom studied in Paris where they had attended the Beaux Arts school, in Rome where they founded an American School, or in Florence, where many opened their own studios. They inaugurated an era of the monumental and the monument.

Their creations can be seen all over the city. These works include the New York Public Library, City Hall, the Metropolitan Museum of Art, Low Library at Columbia University, and many other structures, that while by no means ugly, in many cases may be seen as more monumental than beautiful.

They were concerned not only with buildings, but also city planning. In this regard, they picked up from the work of the previous generation such as Olmstead's creation of Central Park, Riverside Park on the west side of Manhattan, and Prospect and Fort Greene Parks in Brooklyn.

EIRNS/Stuart Lewis

The 42nd Street Library in New York City.

Within this movement, there was a debate between the classical Greek style and the Roman style.

While the "monumental" concerned itself with public buildings, including city halls, courthouses, museums, schools, and universities, the "monument" concerned itself with commemoration of a great leader–military, political, civic, or literary. New York City is filled with such monuments, especially equestrian statues of Civil War generals erected at the expense of old comrades who became men of great wealth following the Civil War.

Many of these statues were set in elaborated squares and plazas, such Grand Army Plaza at the southeast corner of Central Park at the intersection of 59th Street and Fifth Avenue, home to Augustus Saint-Gaudens' magnificent equestrian statue of General William Tecumseh Sherman, and Washington Square Park with its beautiful Triumphal Arch. Another Grand Army Plaza graces the entrance to Prospect Park, Brooklyn, with a complete ensemble of monuments including a Triumphal Arch.

While many of these statues and monuments were executed by some of the best sculptors and architects of the time, and many can be seen on the busy thoroughfares of Manhattan, one monument that is of seminal importance for New York is almost forgotten and never seen by most New Yorkers. It is the Prison Ship Martyrs Monument in Fort Greene Park in Brooklyn overlooking Wallabout Bay, the site of the old Brooklyn Navy Yard. This is the same Fort Greene of the Revolutionary War Battle of New York. Modeled on the commemorative monuments of the Ancient Greeks, it is a single huge Doric column topped by an ancient tripod holding an eternal flame. It stands atop a tomb, the final resting place of many of the 11,500 Americans who died as prisoners of war during the American Revolution. Imprisoned in the rotting hulks of old British warships, their deaths mark the most infamous war crime of His Majesty's Army and Navy, unequaled in that war.

This wanton murder, for murder it was, of more than 11,500 men and women, is more than twice the number of 4,500 revolutionary soldiers who died in battle during the entire Revolutionary War. It is almost four times the number of Americans killed in the World Trade Center. That such a crime is all but forgotten is a

The north face of the Washington Square Arch.

crime in itself, and therefore warrants a telling in this narrative in summary form.

Most of these prisoners were not sailors of the Revolutionary Navy, which hardly existed, but were sailors of privateers and merchantmen captured by the British Navy. By the laws of war, the revolutionary government was not responsible for them. They were not to be released in return for the release of British prisoners. Indeed, British prisoners were highly trained professional soldiers, while many of these seaman were unable even to use firearms.

The British captured and kept them for two reasons:

A warship of His Majesty's navy shared many of the attributes of a prison ship. Much of its crew had been kidnapped by press gangs deployed in English and Scottish harbors. A contingent of Marines was always on board, not so much to fight the enemy as to prevent mutinies by the crew. In times of war, the British Navy was always short of able-bodied seamen. So the idea of imprisoning Americans sailors under horrible conditions was seen as an inducement for them to "join" the navy of the "Motherland." The vast majority, being patriots, refused, for they would rather have died than betray the revolution.

His Majesty's army was even more hard-pressed for manpower. In several battles, including the Battle of Saratoga and especially Yorktown, where the British surrendered, thousands of well-trained, battle-hardened soldiers, irreplaceable at the time, became Washington's prisoners.

By contrast, the British held few revolutionary soldiers as prisoners, because Washington's tactic of fighting, then retreating to fight another day, gave little opportunity to take captives. Manipulating the rules of war, the British therefore simply went out and captured merchant seamen as hostages to trade for British and Hessian soldiers. Washington had to refuse, since such a trade was like giving up battle tanks for jeeps—moreover it would just encourage the British to continue to capture more seamen.

So these poor men, under terrible conditions, faced death. In the prison ship Jersey, known as "Hell" by its inmates, the men died at the rate of ten a day, three hundred per month and 1,200 a year, and were buried in shallow graves on the shore of Wallabout Bay, or simply cast into the deeper waters of the lower Bay of New York.

A poem by J.M. Scott tells the horrid tales of those on the Jersey and the Scorpion:

Let the dark Scorpion's bulk narrate
The dismal tale of English hate
Her horrid scenes let Jersey tell
And mock the shadows where demons dwell.
Their shrieks of pain, and the dying groan,
Unheeded fall on ears of stone.

All Washington could do was to appeal to the humanity, or lack thereof, of the British Commander, General William Howe, to whom he wrote:

You may call us rebels, and say that we deserve no better treatment. But remember, my Lord, that supposing us rebels, we still have feelings as keen and sensible as Loyalists, and will, if forced to it, most assuredly retaliate upon those upon whom we look as the unjust invaders of our rights, liberties and properties.

At the war's end, those who survived left their prisons freer men than when they were captured.

It would be many decades before a fitting grave, let alone a monument would be given to the thousands who perished. Yet even the dead can make their presence felt. As the shallow graves along Wallabout Bay began to expose the bones of the fallen victims, and when the building of the Navy Yard began, the bones were collected—only to be put into barrels and boxes and reburied in the nearby property of John Jackson. Later, with the help of Tammany Hall and concerned citizens, Jackson erected a tomb on his property topped by a memorial, but not of immortal stone, but of easily-perishable wood. And soon it indeed perished, becoming a local eyesore.

It wasn't until 1864 that action was taken, when Fort Greene was transformed into a park and become the site of a real tomb and memorial. Frederick Law Olmstead and Calvert Vaux, fresh from their creation of Central Park, were commissioned to carry out the work. They erected a fitting tomb into a hillside of the park, where the bones were soon transferred. Olmstead and Vaux had planned to top the tomb with a memorial in the popular Gothic style, but this was never done.

It wasn't until 1905 that the firm of McKim, Mead and White, one of the most famous of the "Beaux Arts" firms, was given the commission to create a monument. The task was entrusted to Stanford White, senior partner of the firm. His works included the triumphal arch in Washington Square Park and the nearby Italianate Judson Memorial Church. He was also the architect of Gould Memorial Library at today's Bronx Community College, around which the American Hall of Fame colonnade referenced in Part II of this narrative is located.

As in the Greek classical tradition, White chose a single graceful Doric column topped by a tripod and an eternal flame. At the base of the column were two sculptured eagles executed by Adolph Weinman.

The commemoration of these martyrs was an annual event as part of the Evacuation Day celebrations. The latter commemorated the day—Nov. 25, 1783—when the British finally evacuated New York City. It had been a major yearly celebration in the city up until 1916, after which it was seen as politically incorrect when the United States allied with the British Empire in World War I. Following a refurbishing, in November 2008, a major celebration was held to commemorate the monument's centennial.

Following a campaign led by the Lower Manhattan Historical Society, Bowling Green in Lower Manhattan was co-named "Evacuation Day Plaza, November 25, 1783." The sign was erected on Feb. 22, 2016, George Washington's birthday.

We must return to Athens for an answer to the question of what is a fitting memorial.

By way of introduction: In Prospect Park, Brooklyn, there stands a monument dedicated to the great patriot of freedom, the Marquis de Lafayette. Instead of an equestrian statue atop a pedestal that towers over the viewer, we see a bronze bas-relief executed by the sculptor Daniel Chester French. Rather than mounted on his horse, as if marching into battle, Lafayette stands in a noble pose in front of his horse, overseeing the battlefield. A sense of motion is given to the image by Lafayette's African-American orderly, who struggles with the reigns, as the horse appears to pull his head up in protest. The scene is crested with a blossoming magnolia tree. This orderly is not just a stand-in, but is the slave James Armistead, who also served as Lafayette's spy, especially during the battle of Yorktown. After successfully petitioning the Virginia State Assembly for his freedom, in an effort aided by Lafayette, James took the Frenchman's name for his own.

The work is mounted in a frame of pink granite bas-relief designed by the architect Henry Bacon. The relief columns are inspired by the Tower of Winds in Athens. Unlike the equestrian and other monuments executed in "heroic" style, this memorial exudes a sense of thoughtful understatement, that impels the viewer to reflection rather than over-dramatic awe. It was these two artists, from their studios in New York City, who created the Lincoln Memorial, America's most celebrated monument.

The Prison Ship Martyrs' Monument, at the center of Fort Greene Park in Brooklyn, New York, commemorates the 11,500 American prisoners who died aboard 11 British prison ships during the American Revolutionary War.

New York and the Creation of the Lincoln Memorial

It might be hard to believe that fifty years after the end of the Civil War, there was no monument in the nation's capital to the man who saved the Union, save only for a statue erected in 1868 in front of the District of Columbia City Hall. At the turn of the century, the members of the City Beautiful Movement made the first real efforts to create a memorial. By 1910 Congress had passed the necessary legislation, and in 1911 a Lincoln Memorial Commission was established.

There was already a commission of architects and sculptors, veterans of the City Beautiful Movement, who were busy planning the renovation of Washington D.C., especially the Mall lying between the Capitol building and the White House, where most of the government buildings are concentrated. They strove to revive L'Enfant's original plan. They were called the Fine Arts Commission, and they dominated the proceedings. They included such famous architects as John Russell Pope, who had designed of the National Archives, the Jefferson Memorial and the West Building of the National Gallery of Art. Another member was Charles McKim, senior partner in the famous New York City architecture firm of McKim, Mead, and White. Most were from New York, and were well-known for designing famous museums, and public and university buildings across the country. Yet none of them were chosen to design what would become the most important monument in the United States, which was to be unprecedented in its size and conception. The choice was Henry Bacon.

Known as the "Architect's Architect," Bacon was cut from a different cloth than many of his colleagues in the City Beautiful Movement. Born in Illinois in 1866, the son of a government engineer of old Massachusetts stock, he was raised in North Carolina, where his father was carrying out engineering works for the Army Corps of Engineers. After one year at the university, he left to work as a draftsman and architect in Boston, and then in New York at McKim, Mead, and White. Having won a Rotch Scholarship allowing him to conduct a study tour of Italy, Greece, and Asia Minor, he soon developed a keen interest in classical Greek architecture.

While on his study tour in what is now Turkey, with his brother, Francis Henry Bacon, also an architect and artist, the two brothers married into the Calvert family, consuls for British and American interests in the Dardanelles. The Calverts owned a farm on which the famous site of Troy was discovered by the German entrepreneur and archaeologist Heinrich Schliemann.

During his study tour of Europe, Bacon met another American student, Albert Kahn, who would later found one of the most successful industrial architecture firms in the United states, Albert Kahn Associates. This large firm, which at one time exceeded 600 employees and still exists today, designed Detroit as the nation's "motor city," including many of the automobile factories there. But Kahn also designed graceful institutional buildings in the Neo-Classical and Renaissance styles which brought America's industrial expansion and the City Beautiful Movement together.

Kahn said of Bacon, "to me he proved not only a splendid teacher, but a real friend, whose kindness and stimulating influence I have treasured ever since." This was a sentiment held by all who knew Bacon.

In a time of "Big Industry," and "Big Science," Kahn and the firm McKim, Mead, and White represented "Big Architecture," where one major project could be the work of tens of draftsmen and junior architects, laboring to bring into completion the senior architect's initial idea.

But this was not for Bacon, for one could call him the poet of this generation of architects. For him, architecture was first an art and only second a "career."

After returning to McKim, Mead and White, he soon left to establish his own firm with another archi-

Henry Bacon

tect, James Brite, in 1897. In 1901, Bacon was approached by the Fine Arts Commission to draft plans for a memorial in Washington dedicated to Lincoln. It was in that year that he began to develop his ideas for the memorial, and spent many hours of his own time, so much so that his partnership broke up because Brite could not agree to Bacon's spending so much time on an unpaid project. No matter—Bacon's practice continued to flourish, and he achieved an artist's immortality which Brite never hoped nor sought to achieve.

From the beginning, the Lincoln memorial was intended to be the most important monument in Washington after the Capitol Building and the Washington Monument. It could not be a statue on a pedestal in some overly ornamental setting.

For Bacon, the model was the Parthenon. Not only in its form, but in its very conception. The Parthenon was not conceived like any other temple in the Hellenic world. The temples to Zeus and the other gods were cult centers whose purpose was to propitiate a powerful, and most often a cruel deity, while the Parthenon celebrated Athena, the goddess who gave man the capacity for creating beauty, justice, and wisdom.

Lincoln was no mere "hero" on the battlefield; his qualities and his gifts to the nation went beyond the struggle on the battlefield. The memorial would take the form of a temple celebrating the man who saved the Republic. But it would be more; it would be a temple celebrating that Republic of which Lincoln himself was the personification, like the famous temple to Athena, who was not merely a powerful goddess, but the deity of Hellenic civilization itself. The idea of a memorial to Lincoln being a "Greek Temple" kicked up no little controversy. But what else could it be but a work cast in light of the classical principles of Greece?

Speaking of Greek classical art, John La Farge, a great American artist and decorator, and a friend and collaborator of Bacon, wrote:

That is to say, that they too often do not look to the end, but to the means, while to the artist the means are a mere path—as with the Greeks, whose work will live, even if its very physical existence is obliterated, because it is built in the mind, in the eternity of thought. So Greek art existed, and has lived, and lives, the most flourishing and richest that we know of—with less to represent it than we turn out daily. So it lived, when it had no longer anything of its own body to represent it, in everything that was done in every country which kept its lessons; and lives still, without examples to refer to, even into the very painting of today.

The Lincoln Memorial in Washington, D.C., modeled on the Parthenon.

What other form of art could commemorate Lincoln, who is above all remembered for saving a republic whose principles will live even beyond the life of that republic?

In an interview appearing in the *New York Tribune* on Jan. 7, 1912, Bacon developed his idea:

> The power of impression by an object of reverence and honor is greatest when it is secluded and isolated, for then, in quiet, and without distraction of the senses or mind, the beholder is alone with the lesson which the object is designed to teach and inspire, and will be most subject to its meaning.
>
> This principle of seclusion is an old one. At the height of the achievement in Greece is found the Athena. . . .
>
> The design of the Lincoln Memorial, by withdrawing into the seclusion of a monumental hall the statue of Lincoln and memorials of his two great speeches, and by placing this hall, expressing in its interior the union, in the seclusion of an area surrounded by groves of trees bordered by the Potomac and related to the monument to Washington, will have a significance that is not possible on any other site in the United States.
>
> Terminating the axis which unites it with the Washington monument, it has a significance which no other site can equal, and any emulation or aspiration engendered by a memorial there to Lincoln and his great qualities will be immeasurable, stimulated by being associated with the like feelings already identified with the capital and the monument to George Washington.
>
> On the other end of the axis we have the man who saved that government, and in between the two is the monument to its founder.
>
> All three of the structures, stretching in one grand sweep from Capitol Hill to the Potomac, will lend, one to the others, the association and memories connected with each, and each will have its value increased by being on one axis and having visual relations with the others.
>
> In a vista over two miles long, these three large structures, so placed that they will for ever be free from proximity to the turmoil of ordinary affairs and the discordant irregularity of adjacent secular buildings, will testify to the reverence and honor which attended their erection; and the impression of their dignity and stateliness on the mind of the beholder will be augmented by the surroundings, for which we have free field for symmetrical and proper arrangement.
>
> They are, however, sufficiently far apart for each to be distinguished, isolated and serene, not conflicting in design or appearance the one with the other, and each will impress the observer with the reason for its existence. . . .

The Lincoln Memorial Reflecting Pool in front of the Lincoln Memorial, on a line from the Lincoln Memorial to the Washington Monument (in the background), and the U.S. Capitol.

[The reflecting lagoon adds to tranquility and retirement:]

The Potomac Bridge connects the site with Arlington Cemetery, where the dust of those who gave "the last full increase of devotion" to their country is also a symbol of Reunion. "We are not enemies, but friends. We must not be enemies."—First Inaugural Address....

The Memorial itself should be free from the near approach of vehicles and traffic. Reverence and honor should suffer no distraction through lack of stillness or repose in the presence of a structure reared to noble aims and great deeds.

I propose that the memorial to Lincoln take the form of a monument symbolizing the union of the United States of America, enclosing in the walls of its sanctuary three memorials to the man himself, on a statue of heroic size expressing the human personality, the other memorials of his great speeches, one of the Gettysburg speech, the other of the second inaugural address, each with attendant sculpture and paintings, telling in allegory of his splendid qualities evident in those speeches.

[On Lincoln's statue:]

It will occupy the space of honor, a position facing the entrance which opens toward the Capitol. This position is in a central hold, separated by screens of columns from spaces at each side, in each of which will be one of the other memorials. Each of these three memorial will thus be secluded and isolated, and will exert its greatest influence.

I cannot imagine a memorial to Lincoln so powerful in its meaning and so appropriate to his life as an imposing emblem of the Union, en-

The statue of Abraham Lincoln in the Lincoln Memorial in Washington, D.C.

kernel the memorials of Lincoln's great qualities which must be so portrayed to mankind that Devotion, Integrity, Charity, Patience, Intelligence and Humanness will find incentives to growth by contemplation of a monument to his memory and to the Union the just pride that citizens of the United States have in their country will be supplemented by increasing gratitude to Abraham Lincoln for saving it to them and their children.

The Washington Monument provides enough of the vertical. In the capitol you have the dome effect, and the Lincoln memorial would therefore furnish the horizontal element in a scene of great beauty and historical significance, not conflicting in design and making an imposing whole.

closing memorials of his qualities and achievements.

Each memorial, placed on a site of such significance and possibility of broad treatment as the site in the Potomac Park, will convey its lesson with the greatest of force.

[It is set on a hill:]

On this will rise the memorial to Lincoln, a monument representing the Union he saved by his extraordinary gifts and powers and to which his devotion was supreme.

[The 13 plinths of steps represent the first 13 states; the 36 columns represent the states of the Union in 1865. On the wall of the hall rising above the columns,are the 48 states:]

These three features of the exterior design represent the Union as originally formed, as it was at the triumph of Lincoln's life, and as it is when we plan to erect a monument to his memory.

These cumulative symbols house as their

While Bacon made innumerable journeys to Washington to study the site, the memorial itself was created in New York, not just in its conception and design, but even some of the most important components.

While Bacon designed the "Temple," the statue of Lincoln was created by Daniel Chester French and the often overlooked murals were the work of Jules Guerin, while the dedication behind Lincoln was composed by art critic Royal Cortissoz. All lived and worked in New York City. In fact their offices, studios, and even their homes and social clubs were within walking distances of each other. This area was the Gramarcy Park neighborhood and Greenwich Village. Bacon's office was on 160 Fifth Avenue (the building still stands) at 21st Street, and he apparently maintained his home in the area. French maintained a studio in the area and lived at an address on Gramarcy Park. It is said he created the Lincoln models at the studio of his summer residence, Chesterwood, in Massachusetts, in a home designed by Bacon. Guerin maintained a studio first in the West Village, but later a penthouse studio atop an office building on East 23rd Street and Park Avenue South, and a home on Gramarcy Park a few short blocks from his studio.

Bacon, Guerin, and Cortissoz were members of the Players Club, also on Gramarcy Park, while French was a member of the National Arts Club, which was just next door.

All had worked closely together for many years and enjoyed intimate professional and social relations.

According to one anecdote, Bacon, in the company of his friend and fellow architect Charles Platt, sketched out his ideas for the Lincoln Memorial on the public table at the Players Club. It was Platt who in 1907 designed the town house of Sara Delano Roosevelt, which she shared with her son Franklin; Eleanor Roosevelt described Platt as an "architect of great taste." That house still stands as the Roosevelt Public Policy Institute of Hunter College.

The proximity of their places of work, home, and recreation offered more than mere convenience. At the time, this particular part of Manhattan was the Florence of the United States for the plastic arts. The nation's leading painters and sculptors had their homes and studios in these few square blocks. Even the parks and squares of the neighborhood were the sites of monuments and statues created by the artists in residence. Indeed their works can be seen throughout the squares, parks and museums of New York City, as well as in other cities around the nation.

We often walk the streets of New York, rarely taking a second look at the statues and monuments that adorn the city, and perhaps do not consider them art worth studying. A look at these artists reveals this to be a mistake, because behind each of them is the immortal story of how man struggles, as our Greek author said,

EIRNS/Stuart Lewis

public domain

John Quincy Adams Ward, circa 1900. At top, statue of George Washington in front of Federal Hall in New York City.

"to turn matter into spirit." To infuse a soul into raw stone or bronze.

Many of these artists had undergone training in Paris, Rome, and Florence, tutored by some of the most celebrated artists of the time. Many of the Americans stayed in Europe and expressed themselves in the styles of the impressionism and mannerism popular in Europe at the time. Those who stayed in Europe were often held, perhaps rightly, to have succumbed to the "decadence" of Europe.

But others who assimilated the artistic craftsmanship offered in Europe, returned to the United States with the conviction that the American artist should express himself through American themes. Daniel Chester French was among the latter. They set before themselves the same mission as Poe did for establishing an American literary excellence, but for sculpture and the plastic arts. New York soon became the center of this great mission.

It could be said that French was of the second generation of American sculpture. One of his mentors was John Quincy Adams Ward. (Even Ward's name says something about him.) He is the creator of the statue of Washington that stands before the Federal Building in lower Manhattan. Few could deny that it is a magnificent work of art. It is one of the "American themes" these artists wished to express. Ward depicts Washington stepping forward to take the oath of the office of the Presidency. Washington is not seen in an artificial show of patriotic heroism, ascending to the nation's highest office with all its honor and power. No. Ward reveals the man of great integrity and dignity, who reaches to take the oath, not from ambition, but from a profound sense of responsibility. Ward strives to reveal a certain hesitancy of a man who realizes he is not taking on a new glorious honor, but rather the deep and heavy responsibility of having to preserve the nation he helped to create. Ward strives to bring alive the man, and the hard bronze is transformed into a living memorial.

Ward has not "frozen" Washington, but imparted a sense of motion in solid bronze, as one would "play between the notes" in the performance of a classical musical composition. Sculpture is no different from musical composition or poetry—it is based on the same aesthetic principles that have been practiced since the ancient Greeks more than two thousand year ago. This can be dramatically demonstrated by comparing Ward's "The Freedman," executed in 1862 to commemorate the Emancipation Proclamation, with the Hellenistic "The Boxer at Rest," executed by an unknown master over twenty centuries ago, but only discovered in 1885. Obviously neither artist knew the other nor saw the other's work, but nonetheless they shared the same "poetic principle," as Poe wrote, and managed to create the "in betweenness" so essential for truthful art.

Ward wrote of this work that it was a figure "we call the 'freedman' for want of a better name, but I intended it to express not one set free by any proclamation so much as by his own love of freedom and a conscious power to Brake [sic] things—the struggle is not over with him (as it never is in this life) yet I have tried to express a degree of hope in his undertaking."

Born in 1830, Ward was the protégé of Henry Kirke Brown, born in 1814. The latter's equestrian statue of George Washington can be seen in

Bronze statue of "The Freedman" (1862-63) by John Quincy Adams Ward.

Union Square, Manhattan, and his statue of a standing Lincoln in Prospect Park, Brooklyn, and Union Square in Manhattan. Brown spent four years in Italy, and when he returned, he set up his studio in Brooklyn where he was committed to creating an American idiom for this art.

"The Bison Hunt," by Brown's student, nephew, and adopted son Henry Kirke Bush-Brown, a dramatic depiction of a Native American on horseback slaying a bison, is an obvious Americanization of the classic theme of a man slaying a lion, as in Carl Conrad Albert Wolff's *"Löwenkämpfer"* [Lion Fighter], which stands on the steps of the Altes Museum in Berlin.

New York was fast becoming the Florence or Paris of the United States in its arts and culture. Ward wrote, "The masses of the people, if they don't get the whole of what an artist has expressed, certainly get a part of it. I have never yet seen a really good art work go a-begging in New York. We artists sometimes whine about the lack of appreciation. But in nine out of ten cases the cause of our sorrow lies in ourselves. If a true work of art meets the wants and therefore stirs the feelings of the ordinary human heart, it is sure to win recognition."

Ward's other works can be seen all over New York City, including his "Indian Hunter," "The Pilgrim," "The Sentinel" and "Shakespeare" in Central Park, as well as "Integrity Protecting the Works of Man" on the pediment of the New York Stock exchange of all places.

Needless to say both Brown and Ward deeply opposed slavery.

Ward was French's first mentor. After French studied in Ward's studio for a month, the latter became his lifelong friend and collaborator.

The so-called "Thermae boxer," resting after a match. This Greek bronze statue is of the Hellenistic era (3rd-2nd centuries BC).

The original plaster model by Augustus Saint-Gaudens of the bronze memorial to Robert Gould Shaw leading the first African-American regiment, the Massachusetts Fifty-Fourth Regiment, during the U.S. Civil War. The Bronze memorial is across Beacon Street from the State House in Boston. The model is at the National Gallery of Art in Washington, D.C.

It Is Through Public Monuments that 'We Can Make Our Lives Divine'

Before a discussion of French, I must discuss Augustus Saint-Gaudens, slightly his senior and something of another mentor of French.

Born in Ireland of a French father and an Irish mother, Saint-Gaudens had the passionate personality of his father, who hailed from southern France, and the sensitivity of his Irish mother. His father was a shoemaker by trade, a poor man, and the son grew up on the streets of New York City, engaging in fist fights with the gangs in the neighborhood. Artistically inclined from youth, he took up the trade of a cameo maker, which offered an opportunity to exercise his artistic inclinations, and gave him a modest income to pursue his artistic education, including study at Cooper

Augustus Saint-Gaudens

Union and then in Paris and Rome.

As a young boy, he experienced the political atmosphere of the Civil War, and from the low vantage point of a sidewalk, saw Lincoln's arrival in the city after his election, an image that forever remained with him.

His masterpiece, and one of the most important masterpieces of his time, not only in the United States but internationally, was the Shaw Memorial, dedicated to Colonel Robert Gould Shaw, who led the first African-American regiment to fight in the Civil War. Shaw and many of his comrades fell in battle.

It is a high relief, and while it stands in Boston, it was created in Saint-Gaudens' studio on West 36th Street in Manhattan. While Saint-Gaudens first conceived the project as an equestrian statue, Shaw's parents considered that inappropriate. Although Shaw was brave and fell with honor in battle, he was no Grant or Sherman—therefore it is not for his military exploits he was being commemorated, but for his leadership in leading the first African American regiment in the Civil War.

Saint-Gaudens took this artistic challenge to heart. Shaw is seen mounted on his horse, every bit the leader he was, and behind him in high relief is his regiment of African-Americans. Saint-Gaudens himself said the regiment soon took on more importance than Shaw, or better, the two worked together for a strikingly powerful image.

A project that was originally conceived as a low relief to be completed within a year became a labor of love, which took fourteen years to complete. All of the dozen or so African-American soldiers were modeled from real individuals, some of whom Saint-Gaudens himself recruited from the streets of Manhattan.

The Shaw Memorial was the first public memorial commemorating the heroism of African-Americans in the Civil War.

Saint-Gaudens also created a bust of Sherman from life, which now stands in the Metropolitan Museum of Art, and following Sherman's death, this bust became a model for the artist's great equestrian statue of the General which now stands on the southeast corner of Central Park and Grand Army Plaza on 59th Street and Fifth Avenue.

Born of New England Puritan stock despite his name, French might not have had the passionate personality of Saint-Gaudens, but he shared his unbounded passion for his art. His first commission, the Revolutionary War monument, "The Minuteman," stands in Concord, Massachusetts. After that commission French, like his mentors, left to study in Paris, Rome, and especially Florence. While many of his fellow American art students remained in Europe for their entire careers, French, like Ward and Saint-Gaudens, returned to America to take up the challenge of developing American art through exercising their own creativity. Indeed, the America of the Revolution, the Civil War, and the great economic development and growth of the country demanded an artistic expression.

French soon left Massachusetts and settled among the growing artistic community in New York City, where he began a lifelong collaboration with Bacon, who designed many of the pedestals and settings for his monumental projects, including the Nebraska "Lincoln" and the already-mentioned "Lafayette" in Prospect Park, among many others throughout New York City and the United States. Bacon had done the same for Saint-Gaudens and many others.

Bust of General Sherman by Saint-Gaudens.

This long collaboration made Bacon and French a natural "team" for the Lincoln monument.

While French created his Lincoln, in clay and then plaster, he did not carve it himself. In fact, few sculptors actually carved their works themselves. Mostly professional stone-cutters did the job.

French, like many other sculptors of the time, gave this task to the Piccirilli Brothers and their establishment located in the Bronx. This remarkable establishment had been founded by Giuseppe Piccirilli, a staunch republican and a veteran of Garibaldi's wars of Italian unification, and his six sons. The entire family were not only stone-cutters, but accomplished sculptors in their own right. Theirs was a very New York-style studio. Lunchtime guests often included New York City Mayor Fiorello LaGuardia, with Enrico Caruso singing Neapolitan songs. Their own works and those they carved for others can be seen all over New York City.

These brothers took French's six-foot plaster model of the seated Lincoln, and with the aid of a copying ma-

American sculptor Daniel Chester French. At left: the Minute Man, by Daniel Chester French, erected in 1875 in Concord, Massachusetts.

chine, they transformed the Georgia marble into the monument we see now.

The monument was completed in 1922, after ten years in the making. In 1923, Bacon was awarded the Gold Medal of the American Institute of Architects, which was presented to him by President Harding in a great ceremony on the steps of the Memorial. Within a year he was dead. While earlier virtually unknown outside of his profession, after the completing of the memorial he achieved such fame that thousands attended his funeral at St. Georges Episcopal Church near Gramarcy park. In 1927, a small memorial was erected at the same church.

A tinge of tragedy can be seen in his widow, who lost what ever wealth they held in the 1929 stock market crash. Without children to support her, she was supported by a modest stipend given by the American Institute of Architects.

After Bacon's death, which affected him greatly, French continued the unfinished task of adjusting the artificial lighting of the statue, which took another four years to complete.

The story of Lincoln's Memorial really begins after its completion.

Behind Lincoln's statue is inscribed this epitaph:

IN THIS TEMPLE
AS IN THE HEARTS OF THE PEOPLE
FOR WHOM HE SAVED THE UNION
THE MEMORY OF ABRAHAM LINCOLN
IS ENSHRINED FOREVER

A "memorial" commemorates, while a "temple," as with a house of religious worship, offers the worshipper not only the chance to pay homage to his God, but to draw strength for carrying out his God-given destiny into the future.

In 1939, fourteen years after its completion, the Lincoln Memorial demonstrated its ability to give strength to the those who believed in the great principles upon which our Republic stands, as so effectively declared by Lincoln's Gettysburg Address and Second Inaugural Address, now enshrined in the Memorial.

In that year, forgetting the Revolution they claimed as their parent, the Daughters of the American Revolution denied the right of the African-American contralto Marian Anderson to perform before an integrated audience at their Constitution Hall, the largest auditorium then available in Washington, D.C. At the time Ander-son had just completed a highly successful national tour, giving benefit concerts before integrated audiences in order to raise funds for Howard University.

Eleanor Roosevelt, who had first met the famous singer when she was invited to sing at the White House in 1935, intervened, suggesting that she perform the concert on the steps of the Lincoln Memorial. President Franklin Roosevelt strongly supported it as did Secretary of the Interior Harold Ickes, whose department was responsible for all National Monuments. Ickes himself had been a director of the Chicago chapter of the National Association for the Advancement of Colored People.

To demonstrate that she deplored the DAR's segregationist policy, Eleanor resigned her membership, a move she made public. Fearing she would upstage Anderson, Eleanor chose not attend the concert, but she did persuade the major radio broadcasters to cover it.

On Easter Sunday, 1939 more than 75,000 Americans, representing the entire cross-section of the American population, white and black, young and old, high dignitaries and average working people, gathered to hear Marian Anderson's beautiful yet powerful voice. Anderson opened her concert with *America*, "My country, 'tis of thee, sweet land of liberty," which was followed by operatic classical pieces and a selection of spirituals. She closed it with an encore, the great spiritual "Nobody Knows the Trouble I've Seen."

From that moment on, the Memorial was sanctified. It became and continues to be a temple and shrine for social and political movements seeking to evoke its power in their fight for justice, and the principles upon which the Republic rests, which Lincoln saved. So in the decades since Marian Anderson's concert, the Civil Rights Movement held many demonstrations there, the most memorable led by Martin Luther King, who gave his "I have a dream" speech in 1963 to a gathering of 250,000. But other social movements rallied there as well, especially the anti-war movement against the Vietnam War and other unjust wars.

Daniel Chester French saw the work that assured his immortality for the last time in 1928. Speaking to his daughter on the steps of the Memorial, he asked, "I wonder what they will think of this work a thousand years from now?"

It was a question we may ask ourselves now, at this most historical of junctures. What will they think of our republic, whose temple these artists created, a thousand years from now?

Reviving Classical Culture to Unite Russia, China, and the United States

Below are edited excerpts from an extended discussion in the course of the July 6, 2017 LaRouche PAC National Activists' Call. This call took place one week after the historic Carnegie Hall concert "Tribute to Sylvia Olden Lee—Master Musician and Teacher," and one day prior to the meeting between Presidents Trump and Putin at the G-20 Summit meeting in Hamburg, Germany. Moderating the July 6th discussion was Dennis Speed, of the LaRouche PAC Manhattan Project, and the guests were John Sigerson, the Director of the New York Schiller Institute Chorus, and Bill Roberts and Kesha Rogers, LaRouche PAC National Policy Committee members.

Dennis Speed: In Manhattan last week, several of us participated in a concert that took place at Carnegie Hall exactly a week ago today, and in the aftermath of that concert, there was very informed discussion; there was also a symposium the following day. In the variety of responses to what happened at Carnegie Hall, the characteristic response from everybody that was there (and we've now had scores of responses that are getting into hundreds of responses) was that they thought that they had been changed in some fundamental way. They were transformed, they were moved in some way which was independent of the musical selections. We want to take the opportunity tonight to discuss this, not from the standpoint of the music but from the standpoint of the method of LaRouche which is that which underlies— his conception of the physical economy, his conceptions of science and his conceptions of culture, which are one and the same.

This idea of changing people, of changing the actions of behavior and of thinking—this is the importance of our role and it is indispensable. No other force on the planet, no other group of people seems to be prepared to play that role, and it's what we bring to all of the deliberations and whatever happens programmatically otherwise, that's what our mission has to be. To discuss this, I've requested that we have several people that were there and specifically have not only partici-

pated but directed the process. We want to start tonight with John Sigerson who is the Director of the entire Schiller Institute music program and we'll also be hearing from Kesha Rogers and Bill Roberts a little later. John, go ahead.

John Sigerson: I want to start by just correcting Dennis a little bit. It's not just what we're going to do. We have already, over the past forty years, we have changed the entire climate. Without what we have done over the last forty years, you would not have the Belt and Road Initiative. You would not have what is going on today in China. You would not have what is going on today with Russia. You would not have the potential for us to defeat the Atlantic liberal establishment or the British liberal establishment or "the Blimps," as you might call them. It simply would not have occurred, because we changed people in ways that they did not even know that they changed. We saw that with all of the different things that have happened, including Brexit, including the election of Trump—in which a lot of people who were voting for Trump didn't tell exactly why they were voting for him, but they knew that they had to have something which resonated with them, and that's precisely what we were doing with the music, but also we're doing in general.

I want to say one thing about the concert. I know it's difficult to describe a concert that you were not at, to people around the country, and I wanted to get at that in just one way that might help you.

One of the featured items of that concert was in a certain way the center piece of it—we designed it that way, which is that the great bass-baritone Simon Estes, a towering individual morally and vocally, performed an aria from Verdi's setting of Schiller's play *Don Carlos*, which is a play set in Spain. I just want to say a little bit about that politically because maybe many people may not know that play and what it's all about, but it actually has everything to do with this question of changing people.

This was set in the 16th Century, and this was a dialogue between King Philip II of Spain and an Inquisitor sent by the Vatican, in the wake of the Council of Trent. I don't want to talk a lot about the details, but the Council of Trent was like the Paris environmental agreement that was just made, i.e., it was slamming down and saying, "no development, no nothing"—in this case, anything that is the slightest variation of doctrine of the Church would immediately be prosecuted by the famous Inquisition, which meant torture, which meant the rack, which meant burning at the stake, which meant all sorts of things, if you varied one iota from the line. And that's exactly what the Paris Accords were which Trump has just broken with.

Schiller Institute

The Sylvia Olden Lee Centennial Chorus.

You had the situation in which the King of Spain was fighting wars in the Netherlands in order to crush all of the new religions that were coming up—Lutheranism, Calvinists, all sorts of new religions—but they just wanted to crush the whole thing. You had a figure who was Marquis of Posa, who was invented by Schiller but he was actually very similar to the real character Egmont, and who was a fool ultimately, because he thought he could play a game with the King. He tried to get into the King's confidence and befriend the King in order to fight for what he thought was a loosening up of these laws and a loosening of the Inquisition. The whole thing blew up in his face, as was shown in the dialogue at this concert that was performed, the dialogue between the Inquisitor and King Philip, where it became clear that here is King Philip, he's the ruler of the most powerful nation in the world at that point, and the Inquisitor comes up and crushes him. And you realize he is not in control of anything because what was really in control was much higher.

They force King Philip to break his friendship with Posa, but the deal falls apart, and Posa ends up getting exactly the opposite of what he wanted. Instead of freedom of religion, he ends up sacrificing himself for the weak son of the King, who may have been well intentioned but was not capable of doing anything. It was a true Shakespearean tragedy. If you haven't read the play *Don Carlos*, it's a very good thing to read the Schiller play and then listen to this opera.

What I'm pointing out is that at this critical time, it's very easy—if you want to say there's a moral to this—it's very easy to think that other people are going to make a deal, that somehow somebody else is going to deal with this situation, that somebody else is going to solve these kinds of problems—the higher ups are going to do it, and it's always a fantasy. Because everything relies upon *you* and *your* creative ideas and your creative abilities to solve these problems. Don't rely on any other higher power—the guys up there—they're not going to do it. We see that with the Glass-Steagall, we saw that with the mobilization for JASTA, the Justice Against Sponsors of Terrorism Act, and we see that in music as well.

What we're doing in music is precisely that, it is to get rid of the passivity that has crept into music where people allow themselves to listen to crap, to put it bluntly, and allow relaxing garbage to let them in—of course, a lot of it isn't even relaxing, it's just terrible noise. We're setting up a moral standard for the kind of internal life that you as a human individual, who's responsible for the whole of humanity—you actually feel a resonance lift the fate of all of humanity in a similar way to the way Lyndon LaRouche addresses that and the way I think right now Xi Jinping and Vladimir Putin do feel. I think that there's certainly a resonance of that with Trump. But our job is to reinforce that, as much as possible over this time, not to get diverted and not to think that there's somebody else out there who's going to do this for us. That's our job; it's not Trump's job. It's our job. That's as much as I want to say right now.

Speed: Would you like to say anything at this point, Bill, or do you want to go right to Q&A?

Bill Roberts: Maybe I'll just say something briefly because I had the opportunity to get out during the Fourth of July period; we continue to get an excellent response to our leadership in the population, but as John indicated here, the challenge is that there is a very different reality in the sense of personal responsibility in the American population. Helga Zepp-LaRouche emphasized today that the situation is very, very fragile. There are some excellent things moving forward. There's a great revolution and the potential for peaceful collaboration on the planet, but there are many, many ways that the situation, as it's moving in a positive direction, can fall apart very, very rapidly, and I think the reality is that if the situation is not moved on in terms of a strengthening of this U.S.-China cooperation, something which cannot be done without what Mr. LaRouche has indicated: a Hamiltonian credit system, there are all kinds of ways in which the situation can very, very rapidly devolve. This is really the challenge. I'll just leave it at that for now.

Speed: Kesha? You have something for us?

Kesha Rogers: The real concern around the purpose of this discussion, and what we want to get out of this discussion today, is that it's not a question of music, but it's more a question of the dignity of man, and the idea of what is the responsibility that each and every person on this call and in this nation must start to take on if we're to address the crisis that is confronting the nation. How do you actually start to speak in the way that you remove all practical concerns to say—some people say Glass-Steagall's never going to happen, we're never going to get out of this economic collapse.

When you look at what just took place around the commitment that was put forth by both Russia and China in the recent historic summit that took place a few days ago, the response that was given by China's President Xi Jinping really sets the tone for the very conception of music and harmony among nations that we're talking about and that we actually developed during the concert and tribute of this great genius Sylvia Olden Lee. I want to just say this quickly and then we'll move on.

This is a quote from President Xi Jinping at the summit he had with the Russian President: "We are determined to bolster coordination and cooperation, Russia and international affairs together with the international community, step up efforts to optimize the global governance system to maintain strategic balance and stability throughout the world in order to jointly overcome global threats and challenges of terrorism and to work together to encourage the process of solving conflicts and hot spots through political means in order to form a new type of interstate relation between people based on cooperation and mutual benefit."

What you see coming from this type of mutual cooperation is a real sense of musicality, is a real sense of harmony among nations. What is in the interest, what is going to be to the benefit of every single citizen of each one of those nations? China and the Chinese President have taken up the question of the economic course. That is what we did, that is what was expressed with the development of a true economic chorus in the United States–the basis upon which LaRouche has been building this Manhattan Project. When he first started it, he said he wanted a 1,500-person chorus, not to just make noise and just to sing, but to come together in a way where they—as he made the point—can set people free or get people out of this idea of being practical or complacent, because practical people make stupid people, and they can't think strategically and that's why the music is so important. We can talk more about that, but I'll just say that for now.

Speed: I want to point out something from an article by Lyndon LaRouche which we published in the June 23 issue of the *Executive Intelligence Review*. It's called "The Folly of Chronic War." What he said in this article, which was talking about the problem of the United States or other nations that find themselves in perpetual warfare, "In the great dramas of Shakespeare and Schiller, ... there are no actual heroes in the drama on stage. The hero, as Schiller emphasizes, is the citizen in the audience who is inspired to supply the needed hero of his or her society in oneself, by becoming a true citizen. The same could be said of the tragedies of Aeschylus. For Schiller, an immortal Jeanne d'Arc did not fail, as the history of France in that same century attests, as in the role of Louis XI. Such is the true principle of any really valid Renaissance."

Lyn's idea, put forward there, is that tragedy must be understood as tragedy within this society, not merely in drama. The Central Park enactment of *Julius Caesar* was a desecration of Shakespeare, because what it was advocating was the assassination of the President, yet they didn't say that, but that was what was happening. The conception is that when we look at what is about to happen in the G-20 meeting, we are not innocent bystanders, we're not guilty bystanders either. We're not bystanders. We're people who can actually do something about what is going on that stage.

Question: [A report is given by a participant in the June 29 concert on follow-up discussions with some of the guests, including the powerful impact of the concert on a number of audience members.]

Rogers: Just imagine—and you were there Alvin—but for those on the phone, you have an audience of nearly 2,100 people and a chorus of 220 or 230 people, of all different backgrounds, nationalities, different races, religions, and creeds. The finale of the event was the national anthem, which some people know as the Black National Anthem or the Negro National Anthem. But that song was given a new meaning for the dignity of man and for the question of what it truly means to be human. It was so profound, it was just one of the most moving parts of the performance.

As everyone rose from their seat, you could see the whole audience and chorus start singing together in unison. The words to the song start, "Lift every voice and sing till Earth and Heaven ring, ring with the harmonies of liberty." You think about that and how that really set a tone within the hearts and minds of the people who were participating, that there's so much division happening in the world right now, that for the first time they saw that as a song that unified. Many people know that song as, "Oh, that's what you sing in February because it's the Black National Anthem, and it's for the Black people to sing." But that's not what it's about. The conductor Roland Carter made that point very clear. It's a song of harmony, of the interest of all humanity.

What's important to communicate here is the power of the poetry in the music, what Sylvia Olden Lee, the great first Black female musician, vocal coach, and pianist with the Met, whom we were honoring for her one hundredth birthday, insisted upon. What is more important than just how nice someone can sing, the beauty of the voice, the beauty of the music itself, is how well it can communicate the poetry—how well they were able to get into the mind of the poet and the artists to be able to convey that through music to touch the hearts and minds of those whom they were communicating to, singing to.

This is so important, because this is what is our responsibility is right now is that what we have to do in the midst of such trauma, such turmoil, such chaos that's happening in society, the culture of violence. You know you see all these efforts trying to call for Trump's assassination, the culture of rapping, violence that's feeding in the streets. If you don't have something that is going to grab the hearts and souls of the population and move them—you may feel that they're not even ready for it. You might think you brought friends to the concert, and maybe they were a little bit out of it, but despite that, they were touched in a way that they had to go back and think about it. Everyone who came to that concert and more so, everyone who's coming in and encounters the Schiller Institute, the LaRouche organization, is having to rethink what it is as their purpose and mission and meaning of life, and the music always helps you convey the ideas through that, really helps you to understand what it is that is the responsibility of each and every person to take on, as a part of a process of changing, of a harmonic process, not just your own personal responsibility to yourself, but your responsibility to others, to the rest of humanity. I think we can take from this moment, that the potential right now is somewhat uncertain, but at the same time, it's very great, and it's something that we all should be very happy to take the challenge of.

Sigerson: I'd like to add something. When Lyndon LaRouche many, many years ago first met Helga Zepp, they went for a walk. I think it was in Berlin, and on this walk, Lyndon said something to Helga which completely changed her life, which was, "Are you willing to feel responsible for the fate of all humanity? Can you do that in your heart? Can you feel responsible, can you *be* responsible and act in the way that is responsible for all of humanity?" It was that, I know, that recruited, in many more ways than one, Helga to the Lyndon La-

Lyndon H. LaRouche, Jr.

Rouche movement. I would just say yes, indeed, to what Kesha just said on that question of personal responsibility, just to quote the last stanza of *Lift Every Voice and Sing,*

> Lest our feet stray from the places, our God, where
>   we met Thee,
> Lest our hearts, drunk with the wine of the world,
>   forget Thee;
> Shadowed beneath Thy hand,
> May we forever stand,
> True to our God,
> True to our native land.

Speed: There were over two hundred people in the chorus—there are two hundred responses right there. And then you have the people that they brought; that's another two to three hundred responses. And just for everybody who's listening, just for an idea of what we're getting at here: look: We get on these phone calls on Thursdays and Mondays. We have basically about one hundred-fifty to two hundred people. Then we have the additional people on the internet, so about three hundred people roughly are participating as we speak, either immediately on the phone calls, or just after the phone call. Sometimes it goes way up, in the course of a week, to one thousand, or something like that.

Now, people say: Well, wait a minute. There are 350 million people in the United States, so how does this really go anywhere? How is it getting there?

Well, the point of chorus, the idea of the chorus—you heard that Kesha used the term the "economic chorus." You see, you can change the entire direction of the United States if you've got a few hundred people, let alone a few thousand people, in chorus, all talking about, or singing and displaying their voices behind the same idea, the same force. And what we were doing there, without making too much of an analogy, I don't want to make this too mechanistic, but I just want you to know what we're really discussing here is the power of ideas. That you can take an idea which is *right*, and if you place it in the right way in your voice, and you place it at the right time in a society, that idea will become the hegemonic, dominant conception, no matter what kind of powerful force tries to stop it.

Let me repeat that last part: No matter what powerful force tries to stop it, that idea will become the dominant idea in the society if you can place it in the proper voicing and you place it at the proper time. Now, we're in that kind of time, right now. The Presidency of the United States right now is capable, of expressing, through *our* voice such an idea. But we've got to be very clear, and the reason it's important was the overall discussion here. We're not talking about music—if you got on the call late you might not know what we're doing.

But I just want people to understand that we have a power in the LaRouche operation; it's one of these things that we really are trying to struggle to get across. A lot of the time, it's not the particular program, it's not the particular campaign we're doing, not the particular things we're saying. It's not that. It's the intent and the placement of the greatness of the idea of humanity. Humanity is great. Humanity is great because it can do something that no other species is known to be able to do: it can transform its own axioms,– thinking and behavior—and can transform the universe as a result, physically. And the celebration of that is what you have as what's called culture.

It's not a form, it's not foreign to anybody. It's the way *you are*, already. Humanity is this way. Now that doesn't mean it behaves that way—I didn't say that. I don't mean, if you look around at humanity today, you can tell it's all great, although you can see instances of greatness in China and Russia, and a few other places.

As we go into the next questions, you can ask anything; don't feel that you have to only ask about the particular things, but we want you to understand the reason—we're very excited, those of us who participated or organize here in Manhattan—it's because we recognize that we had done something that went way beyond anything we planned. This was a fundamental transformation. We didn't plan that, we hoped for it. But it actually happened. And it shows the power of playing the right idea in the right voice.

Question: This is S. from Indiana. We're looking at the G-20 summit going on this weekend and we have Trump over there representing the American people. I just want to remind people that Trump is supposed to represent us, which means that he should be taking the lead from us, the people, which means that we have to make known what is really necessary, which through the LaRouche movement is making big waves. We just need to remember it's the American people that are supporting what their public servants do, and that Trump won his election to make America great, to rebuild America; that means infrastructure, economy.

Question: This is G. from Miami. How do we go about getting an infrastructure bank in our country to bring us into the 21st Century, and have the enjoyment of the velocity of dollars for Americans?

Roberts: We're at the point at which if we don't get these projects going, you're going to have millions and millions of Americans out of work, you're going to have a shutdown of transportation in New York City. I'm positive there are discussions of this type on how this is going to be done between the Chinese and various CEOs. This is so immediate; in a sense we just have to move, very, very rapidly, and impress upon people the urgency of this situation.

But we know how to do it.

Speed: We have a conference tomorrow at the Kaufman Center in New York, and there will be a delegation from China who will be at our conference, in force. I was with them today at the United Nations. What was going on with them, is a total fight, and the fight was made very clear actually by two exchanges: One was by Dr. Pat Ho, of the China Energy Fund Committee, and the other was one of the representatives from a particular corporation from China. And in Patrick's presentation, he talked about the problem of Thomas Malthus and Malthusian economics, and he referenced the Club of Rome, an organization from the 1970s and '80s, which is only concerned about limiting population growth. And he compared that to an individual by the name of Julian Simon, who did famously challenge the "Limits to Growth" outlook.

The other individual who spoke—I won't go through particulars—referenced someone by the name of Lester Brown, very well known to those from the LaRouche camp. Lester Brown was from the Worldwatch Institute, and that organization was always talking about the catastrophe of overpopulation, how there would be such a woeful situation because Mexico has too many people and China has too many people. So this speaker, who was Chinese, remembered having had a personal conversation with Lester Brown, and Lester was telling him, "how are we going to feed the Chinese, when you get to the 21st Century?" And this individual said, "Well, when Lester Brown was telling us that, at that time there were roughly 700 million people in China. Now there are 1.4 billion people in China. At this time, we are now food self-sufficient. *We* have fed the Chinese, the Chinese fed the Chinese. And in addition to that, half of the grain that we produce in our country, feeds animals." So this was his way of basically stating that human ingenuity and the approach of the Chinese solved the problem.

Now, when we get on the phone here, and talk about things like infrastructure banks or things like that, let me tell you something: This is *child's play* for the United States. The United States was the most productive economy in human history! The reason that the United States decayed and is nonproductive was not because it didn't know what to do financially or economically or agriculturally. It was because of the rock-drug-sex-counterculture which was consciously and deliberately created by elements of the Central Intelligence Agency, and British intelligence, starting in the mid-1950s: Robert Gordon Wasson who was the vice president of JP Morgan Bank, was the first person to visit Mexico and write an article in *Life* magazine which pushed the idea of the so-called "magic mushroom," psilocybin.

I reference it, because the entire hippy counterculture of the 1960s based itself, and said it dates itself, from the issuance of that article in the *Life* magazine. It was the Luce family, as in Henry Booth Luce and Clare Booth Luce, of *Time* magazine—they, first of all, were LSD users themselves. But they promoted it through Madison Avenue.

I say this, because this idea that some particular thing, or project, or way or bank, or means, or mechanism, or program, or policy, or rule—*this is crap*!

The United States *knows how to do this*. The problem is, that the people are terrified and harassed and harangued against the Presidency of the United States, as their vehicle. It's what John said earlier: *We* are the Presidency of the United States, not Donald Trump. He is *also* the Presidency of the United States, but we've been part of the Presidency, in the case of our movement in particular, ever since the late 1970s, actually, and the early '80s, when Lyn played a particular and central role, as the back channel to the then-Soviet Union.

So, we're saying that because you should have more confidence, and you also should just state the ugly truth: The last sixty years of American history was completely unnecessary! It didn't have to happen this way at all, and it was done by seizing the culture, taking the cultural road, and brainwashing the American people, and the American people capitulated to it.

Now, we're not blaming people for that. Our approach is that we know best, we know what to do. Get into our movement, and we can do the opposite. But just so we have a clarity about this, so that you all have it: The truth is, we are going to be able through the Trump Presidency, to change the country, and to change it in a fundamental way. And the small stuff? Don't sweat the small stuff.

Sigerson: Can I just add something? I think that everybody on this call has to stop thinking "why can't this be done? Why isn't this being done? Why isn't so and so doing this?" and similar types of questions. Again: You have to know that even thinking that way is actually a sign of the cultural pessimism which has taken over the United States over the past generation: This is what Dennis was talking about. You have to look into your own mind and root out those kinds of thoughts, because actually they're destructive thoughts, in a certain way. You never just say, "why isn't something happening, why can't this happen? Why can't that happen?" The point is, you know what has to happen. And you just make it happen. And you can be *happy* that way. You're much happier doing it that way, than sitting around worrying about why isn't this happening?

Believe me.

The New Silk Road Becomes the World Land-Bridge

The BRICS countries have a strategy to prevent war and economic catastrophe. It's time for the rest of the world to join!

This 374-page report is a road-map to the New World Economic Order that Lyndon and Helga LaRouche have championed for over 20 years.

Includes:

Introduction by Helga Zepp-LaRouche, "The New Silk Road Leads to the Future of Mankind!"

The metrics of progress, with emphasis on the scientific principles required for survival of mankind: nuclear power and desalination; the fusion power economy; solving the water crisis.

The three keystone nations: China, the core nation of the New Silk Road; Russia's mission in North Central Eurasia and the Arctic; India prepares to take on its legacy of leadership.

Other regions: The potential contributions of Southwest, Central, and Southeast Asia, Australia, Europe, and Africa.

The report is available in PDF $35 and in hard copy $50 (softcover) $75 (hardcover) plus shipping and handling.

Order from http://store.larouchepub.com

The Sylvia Olden Lee Concert Tribute Reverberates

by Dennis Speed

July 11—The Schiller Institute New York City Chorus, as well as other participants in the June 29 concert, spoke and corresponded with audience members afterwards. Here is a sample taken from the several hundred responses. They reflect, not merely "reactions to music," but deeper considerations that go to the heart of the intent behind the Schiller Institute, the Foundation for the Revival of Classical Culture, and the Harlem Opera Theater's joint collaboration and mission to form a 1500-person chorus in New York City.

From an elder Chinese musician (translated):

I was very impressed with the duet and multi-part singing, and particularly the chorus. They coordinated so well. A high level performance. The whole concert was a composition.

From two members of the Flushing, Queens chapter of the Schiller Institute chorus:

We invited sixteen friends to come to the concert. They were excited as we, their friends and very common people, appeared and participated in the great performance on the stage of Carnegie, one of the greatest music holy lands of the world. They are all music-lovers, and many of them love Classical music. They (were) amazed at the great performance of the high-level Italian opera and Classical music soloists. But they loved the African-style spiritual more, as it opened their eyes, and they think it is so beautiful and touching…. However, they loved our singing best, as so many people, including us, sang together to create (such) harmonious great music. To them, the effect was shocking! (We) feel good as our friends loved our choir as well

as our performance. We were treated as heroes with 'Hail!' and flowers, although we are just small potatoes, and contribute only a little to the group.

Thank you very much for your help and the chance to have this great experience.

From a concert organizer, who helped bring members of a Buddhist temple to the concert:

14 people: five monks, three parents, and six children came from the Buddhist temple. None, except the lead monk, even knew what Carnegie Hall was, so this was huge. They were very excited. They told me that there was a lot they did not understand, but they loved the duet from *Don Carlos,* and especially the chorus. Their commitment to the singing process vastly increased.

From a chorus member:

I received a "Thank You" card from former concert pianist, who does not speak English, with a $100 check inside!

From a professional singer:

What a magnificent evening, and I can tell Sylvia Olden Lee was a very special person as well as a genius teacher, singer, and musician, from all I heard and saw at the concert!

(I was) so impressed with what was organized and yes, I am very fascinated even more now about the Schiller Institute as the special choir was *outstanding!*

Thanks for our chat, your contact information. So sorry I can not attend the Symposium tomorrow. I hope it is very well-attended and perhaps it can be recorded or such.

You are terrific and I have included my contact information.

You will see, humbly, if you Google me—especially if you put "soprano" after it—that I am quite well known. . . .

From a trombonist friend of conductor Diane Sare, who sang in the bass section:

Congratulations on a brilliant concert! Your conducting was exceptional, and the spirit of the evening was powerful. My heartfelt thanks for including me in this special event. After singing this evening I am thoroughly convinced of the validity of natural tuning (as if Corelli weren't enough). Please let Frank (Mathis) know I was deeply moved by his Roland Hayes interpretation, and he held his own in the Donizetti with some heavy hitters, too!

From a retired singer, now re-activated:

I want to thank you for the great opportunity to sing again like last night at Carnegie Hall.

Since 2006, (when) I sang *Carmina Burana* by Carl Orff (I did) not sing any more until I met the Schiller institute choir at Christmas of 2016. . . .

I had thought not to return to the choir due to personal reasons. But, after last night, I just want to sing again like the "Tenor" I was 19 years ago (or maybe better). . . . I have no words to thank you for this new opportunity, I hope I don't disappoint you.

Thank you very much.

Ambassadors to the United Nations, heads and former heads of engineering and science organizations, and other officials, including the office of the Mayor of New York City and New York State Assembly and Senate offices also attended the concert.

New York City Can Learn a Lesson From the Oroville Dam Catastrophe

by Patrick Ruckert

July 7—On June 29, just days after a subway derailment in New York City that injured 34 people and did substantial damage to the tunnel, New York State Governor Andrew Cuomo signed an executive order declaring a state of emergency for the Metropolitan Transit System. In California, the Oroville Dam spillway collapsed in February and threatened a catastrophic flood, forcing 180,000 people to flee for their lives. There are hundreds of potential infrastructure disasters just as dramatic, or even more so, across the length and breath of the nation.

As *EIR* has reported, and demanded, again and again, the President must hear a loud and clear call from the American people, that nothing less will work, than enacting a full, Hamiltonian credit system to fund $2 trillion to $3 trillion per year for repairing and building the nation's infrastructure, and creating a new platform of productive economic development. It certainly is not enough to repair the nation's broken-down infrastructure; not when entire systems like the New York City transit system are beyond repair.

While California's water management system 40 years ago was the envy of the world, it can no longer provide the water required by a population that today is twice as large as it was then. And, as the Oroville Dam spillway collapse demonstrates, at least parts of the system are falling apart. That incredible system was the first in the world to unite multiple watersheds and river systems into one coherent water delivery machine. Now a new platform for the entire continent is required—one that creates a unified, continental water management system, as the proposed North American Water and

Power Alliance (NAWAPA) would do. You want a real job? There will be several million jobs, lasting 25 years, building NAWAPA. (See the NAWAPA XXI Animated Overview.)

It is not enough to show people a list of projects that are of urgent necessity. That list is decades old, and gets longer every year. The American people must be awakened once again to a great spirit of adventure and mission, like that which grabbed them and propelled the Apollo Project to the Moon.

Decades of destruction of America's physical economy, as the parasites of Wall Street turned the nation into a gambling casino—and the concomitant virtual obliteration of any sense in our people that they

William Croyle/California Department of Water Resources

An aerial photo shows the damaged spillway and eroded hillside at Oroville Dam.

are important because they contribute to building, growing, and manufacturing all that we all require to live and what the future requires—has produced the fatal illusion in the minds of too many, that "Nothing can be done. It will never work. They won't let us do it."

That mind-set must end now. The useless and futureless "jobs" most younger people have today, are not a condition created by God. So, grab your future in your own hands, and join with the LaRouche political movement to awaken our fellow citizens to their responsibilities: Blast the Hell out of every elected official and others, until they join the campaign to really make America great again by enacting that Hamiltonian credit system that will open the doors to undertaking one great project after another.

Oroville, New York City, the Nation

What is accepted as today's reality can be changed in a minute. So, let's look at one of those "minutes" that changes everything, and there we will find that once-sacrosanct procedures, laws, regulations and even financing limitations, can and will die when it is necessary that they do so.

My article in the March 3, 2017 issue of *EIR*, "Oroville Dam's Near Catastrophe: A Wake Up Call for the Nation," began with this:

Late Sunday afternoon on February 12, an emergency alarm was sounded by the Yuba County California Sheriff:

"This is an evacuation order. Immediate evacuation from the low levels of Oroville and areas downstream is ordered. A hazardous situation is developing with the Oroville Dam auxiliary spillway. Operation of the auxiliary spillway has led to severe erosion that could lead to a failure of the structure. Failure of the auxiliary spillway structure will result in an uncontrolled release of flood waters from Lake Oroville. Immediate evacuation from the low levels of Oroville and areas downstream is ordered. This is NOT A Drill. This is NOT A Drill. This is NOT A Drill."

Soon, 188,000 people were in their cars, jamming the roads and becoming more and more panic stricken as authorities were warning over emergency broadcast networks, that the Oroville Dam emergency spillway could collapse within the hour. Had it done so, a 30-foot wall of water would have swept down the valley of the Feather River. The casualties would have been in the thousands.

For those 188,000 people, that day was terrifying. For millions in New York City, the prospect of finding themselves stuck in a broken-down subway car is terrifying. Meanwhile, even the ability to get to work in the morning has become a crap-shoot.

The near-catastrophe in California began when, on February 9, the spillway of Oroville Dam began disintegrating, sending huge chunks of concrete and millions of tons of earth and rocks into the Feather River below the dam. The Oroville Dam is the tallest dam in the nation at 770 feet, and is a lynchpin of the entire California water management system that provides water to nearly 30 million people and irrigates millions of acres of the nation's most productive farmland.

Immediately, the water-flow down the damaged spillway was stopped, and the water level in the reservoir behind the dam began to rise. Then it overflowed into the emergency spillway, which had never been used in the fifty-year life of the dam. Three days later, as it became clear that the foundation of the emergency spillway was being undermined by the water-flow, threatening to collapse it, the emergency evacuation order was issued. Only by opening the gates of the damaged spillway once again was the immediate danger alleviated.

Tear Up All the Rules

While the Oroville Dam spillway collapse has been a wake-up call which demonstrates that ignoring the nation's deteriorating infrastructure for decades guarantees that disaster will strike, it is what has happened since at the dam, that provides us with another wake-up call, this one demonstrating how the rebuilding of the nation must be done.

What has occurred in the six months since the dam's spillway broke, goes far beyond the streamlining of regulations called for by President Trump. The entire regulatory structure of the state and federal governments has been thrown in the garbage can, including the normally required and usually obnoxious environmental-impact statements. There have been no years-long studies of the problem, no drawn-out court battles delaying construction, and no bureaucratic or other delaying actions allowed by the legislature, the

Congress or anyone else.

That spillway must be repaired and repaired fast, before the rainy season begins in October. And so the announcement, bidding, and awarding of the construction contract process, which normally takes years, was done in less than two weeks. The actual construction work to repair the spillway began in early May, after more than two million tons of rock and dirt, which had washed into the Feather River, had been removed. That job had been done on a 24 hours a day, seven days a week schedule.

The construction contract to rebuild both the broken spillway and the emergency spillway was awarded to the Kiewit Corporation, an internationally renowned contractor for big jobs. As many as 500 workers, dozens of pieces of heavy equipment, a large fleet of trucks, and two concrete plants built on site, are now working 20 hours per day, six days a week, to get the first phase completed by October 1.

Earlier, on April 12, as reported by the *Chico Enterprise-Record*, Bill Croyle, State Department of Water Resources Acting Director, said that normally, a project of this size would take years just for the planning. "We need hours and days for approval vs. weeks, months and years," he said. Rather than have paperwork shuffle back and forth, staff from agencies will meet together, Croyle said.

Having already spent over one-quarter of a billion dollars in removing the debris, the repair job contract adds another $275 million, putting the total over $500 million. That does not include the costs of repairing other damages resulting from the emergency that are not directly related to the dam.

From where would that money come? Virtually out of thin air. It certainly had not been budgeted. The Governor, Jerry Brown, requested emergency funds from the Federal Emergency Management Agency (FEMA)

Concrete reinforcement being applied to the emergency spillway of the Oroville Dam during the crisis at the dam in 2017.

for repairing the spillway and other infrastructure damaged by the Winter storms. On April 2, the Trump Administration announced that the President had approved federal aid to California of $274 million for Oroville Dam repair and other needs.

Who in the Congress is saying that what is being done at Oroville Dam, should be done for the New York City subway and train system, and another hundred similar potential disasters all around the nation? Not a one of them. Do we hear that from the Trump Administration? Not yet. How about from the American people? If not terrorized by 20 years of hell and destruction that our own government has hit them with, perhaps they are numbed by the drugs and entertainment they ingest.

So what? We have the example of Oroville Dam, so let us use it to shake them all to life once again.

As we have seen in the Oroville Dam case, when something must be done, neither money, nor the EPA, nor the permitting and bidding process will be allowed to hold back getting the job done.

That is the spirit required to rebuild the nation. That is the new wake-up call for the nation from the Oroville Dam emergency.

The Truths Driving China's Banking System Today

by Brian Lantz

July 8—China's Belt and Road Initiative now encompasses at least seventy nations. Launched in 2013, the greatest engineering project in the world is being built across Eurasia and into Africa, and now reaches the Americas. More than seventy nations, encompassing 4.4 billion people, are now engaged. Now being built are high-speed rail networks, new ports along the coasts of Eurasia and African nations, new rail and highway routes linking the capitals of Africa, large-scale water reclamation and hydro-electric projects, communication connectivity including satellite networks, and new universities and science cities.

Japan is joining with Russia to develop Russia's Far East. Eastern European cities are becoming hubs of north-south, east-west transport, and Eurasia is being integrated.

Financing is being generated through a new financial architecture, as recently endorsed by the Group of 20 nations. President Trump has stated that the United States will now cooperate with China's Belt and Road Initiative. The U.S. Chamber of Commerce agrees. Where did all of this come from?

This article will take the reader inside China's banking *and credit* system. However, to understand what is occurring in China today, and its Belt and Road Initiative open to all, is also to provide a platform for rediscovery of the motive force at the root of the Massachusetts Bay Colony's Pine Tree Shilling system of three hundred sixty-five years ago. To make that discovery, a vicarious hypoth-

esis is required![1]

As Helga Zepp-LaRouche presented in her speech, "East and West: A Dialogue of Great Cultures," in New York City on April 13 of this year,[2] there is indeed something profound and universal belonging to all cultures. In the West, we know this as the republican system for the common good. "It considers all people as capable of the potentiality endless perfection, and sees it as the duty of the state to promote, in the best possible way, the creative capability of its citizens"—as, for example, embodied in the General Welfare Clause of the U.S. Constitution, but also in the dynamic of today's China.

In that same speech, Zepp-LaRouche quoted Friedrich Schiller from his writings on the sublime: "All

---

1. *To: International Economic Policy: The Great Ontological Paradox*, by Lyndon LaRouche, July 12, 2013, *EIR* Vol. 40 No. 27.
2. Helga Zepp LaRouche, Whither the U.S.: Nuclear War or New Silk Road?, EIR, Vol. 44 No. 16.

Xinhua

The Doraleh Multi-Purpose Port, an addition to the Port of Djibouti, was constructed by China State Construction Engineering Corporation (CSCEC). The opening ceremony was on May 24, 2017. For now, it is the largest port project by Chinese construction companies in northeast Africa.

Statues of Confucius and Friedrich Schiller.

other things *must*; man is the being who *wills*. ... The Morally educated man, and only this one, is entirely free. Only the person who has a beautiful character, who finds joy in exercising justice, well-being, moderation, steadfastness, and devotion; and whoever doesn't lose these qualities even if hit by an array of great misfortunes, is sublime."

And then Confucius from his book *The Great Learning—Daxue*: "The highest knowledge is that reality is impacted; Only when it engages has reality reached its height. Then ideas become true; only then is the consciousness just. Only when the consciousness is just, will the person be educated. Only if the person is educated, if the home is regulated and the state governed, is there peace in the world."

More Hamiltonian than America?

Before proceeding to the meat of this article, a great irony must be made explicit, and one which perhaps American leaders will take to heart today. That irony, is that everything which has been accomplished in the Chinese economic miracle is fully coherent with the principles of economics defined by America's first Treasury Secretary Alexander Hamilton, and in some instances this is explicit. This has been done while under the sixteen years of George Bush and Barack Obama, the Hamiltonian outlook has been practically eradicated from public life in the United States.

Take the decision, in 1993, to impose the equivalent of Glass-Steagall banking separation on the then-troubled Chinese banking system. This was done, as several sources have reported, to focus the resources of China's banking institutions on productive investment and to dry up financial speculation. This is exactly what Franklin Roosevelt did. It worked in the United States for sixty years, and then it was repealed in 1999. Now China has resurrected this approach.

Take, also, China's accomplishment in lifting 700 million of her own people out of poverty, and recognize that this was the paramount goal—the intention—of the banking reforms from the beginning. China's banking reforms were never merely "monetarist"; they are not just about money and finance. Everything China has done, has been driven by an unshakeable commitment to build up the productive economy and to uplift the people: to further the *General Welfare*, as Hamilton would put it—or the *People's Livelihood*, as Sun Yat-sen would put it—of the Chinese people.

Look also at the density and complexity of the reforms described below. Things were tried and discarded; there has been a great deal of flexibility in China's approach, but what is ironclad—*axiomatic*—is the notion of a *Public Credit System.* The success of that vision is readily apparent both in the stupendous development of China internally, as well as in the now radiating effects of the Belt and Road initiative.

If China can do this, why can't the United States?

What is 'Reform and Opening Up'?

Since the denouement of the "Cultural Revolution" and overthrow of "the Gang of Four," China has gone through a moral and spiritual reawakening, not unlike that which the European Renaissance brought into being out of the civilizational crisis of Europe's 14th Century systemic collapse and resulting "Black Death."

Starting with paramount leader[3] Deng Xiaoping's announcement of China's "reform and opening up," the

---

3. Deng Xiaoping was neither the President nor Premier of China; nor was he the the Communist Party head. By consensus, he had come forward, and been recognized as the "paramount leader" in that time of crisis.

Deng Xiaoping (center) and his wife Zhuo Lin (right of him) being briefed by Johnson Space Center director Christopher C. Kraft (right front) on Feb. 2, 1979.

nation has taken itself along a path of non-linear leaps, including dramatic decisions in developing its State-directed, dirigist financial system. Proposals to create a western "central bank," as modeled on the U.S. Federal Reserve, have been firmly rejected. Deeply-held Confucian precepts regarding wise leadership—like those which underlay Alexander Hamilton's design of a national credit system—do not allow for privatized, Hobbesian methods of decision making. These decisions are not mere ideology.

The evolving mission-requirements of taking a "Third World" country of 1.4 billion people into the 21st Century, and simultaneously leading a global infrastructure renaissance, are beyond daunting. A multi-generational perspective is required—to think as if you already stood fifty to one hundred years in the future. China's President and its Premier, the Standing Committee of the State Council (the chief administrative authority of China's government), the National Development & Reform Commission, and the important "Leading Groups" spearheading vital initiatives, are among the most remarkably compact and collaborative decision-making bodies in existence anywhere.

They are making the strategic decisions, and working to publicly provide inspiration and direction, set goals, and evolve needed structures. They draw on China's burgeoning science institutions, think-tanks, and universities. China's "Made in China 2025" initiative, to create "Industry 4.0," was drafted over a period of years by the Ministry of Industry and Information Technology (MIIT) with the input of one hundred fifty experts just from the Chinese Academy of Engineering. China's universities will graduate eight million students in 2017, twice that of the United States. Again, from Confucius: "Only if the person is educated, if the home is regulated and the state governed, is there peace in the world."

Today, China's banking system is a multi-tiered system with its own still-evolving set of checks and balances. Outlined below are important aspects of China's dynamic financial system, bearing on potential China-United States collaboration in creating a required new global financial architecture. As the reader will see, there have been many growing pains and much problem-solving along the way.

People's Bank of China—Out of Wartime Conditions

The People's Bank of China (PBC) carries out many of the necessary functions of a "western" central bank, with responsibility for China's currency policy, bank-clearing functions, foreign exchange reserves ($3.1 trillion), and a role in oversight of the macro-economy. The history is more profound. On Oct. 1, 1949, when the People's Republic of China was declared, the core of the People's Bank had already been brought into existence, created as the new government administrative agency which printed—and worked to stabilize—a new currency, the Renminbi (literally "the People's currency"), while simultaneously acting to attract and allocate funds to make reconstruction of China possible.

In short, the PBC was first the government's "bookkeeper and cashier," allocating resources, while it was also utilized to fill both commercial bank and "central bank" functions for the People's Republic in its relations with the world.

It was in the 1978 "reforms and opening up," following the disaster of the "Great Leap Forward" and benighted "Cultural Revolution," that China's new emerging leadership initiated a two-tiered, state-owned banking system reform at the center of the nationwide reform. Here one must resist, and step outside London's and Wall Street's monetarist straightjacket, and rationally reflect on Alexander Hamilton's actual design of—and President Washington's and Congress' support for—a sovereign national credit system, this under conditions of continued warfare with a now-global British Empire.

Recall the lessons derived by the great German historian, poet and playwright Friedrich Schiller from the tragic outcome of the French Revolution, reported in the Third Letter of his *Aesthetic Letters:*

> The great deliberation is therefore, that the physical society may not cease in time for a moment, whilst the moral form itself in the idea, that existence may not fall into danger for the sake of the dignity of man. If the artisan hath to repair a clockwork, so he lets the wheels run down; but the living clockwork of the State must be repaired whilst it strikes, and here it means, to exchange the rolling wheel [for another] during its revolution. One must therefore search for a support for the continuance of society, which makes it independent of the natural State, which one wants to dissolve.

Deng Xiaoping carefully commented on the missteps made by the Communist Party of China (CPC) prior to and during the 1966-1976 Cultural Revolution:

Wikimedia/Brücke-Osteuropa

Roadside billboard of Deng Xiaoping at the entrance of the Lychee Park in Shenzhen.

"The past mistakes indeed owed to some individual leaders' thoughts and working styles, but the imperfect organizational schemes and structure played bigger roles."

Building further on the 1978-era reforms, China created three new "policy banks" (*zhengce yinhang*) in 1994, under the direct leadership of China's State Council, as the vehicles for direct government policy initiatives. PBC policy, under the direction of then Vice Premier Zhu Rongji, was shifted to indirect control: interest rates, reserve funds deposit rates and open markets. Today important independent regulatory agencies exist under the umbrella of the PBC, which the body of this article will refer back to:

• Since 1978, the State Administration of Foreign Exchange (SAFE), which is responsible for monitoring, supervising and proposing reforms bearing on the nation's foreign reserves, as well as for "operations and management of foreign reserves, gold reserves, and assets of the state."

• Since 2003, the China Banking Regulatory Commission (CBRC), which is responsible for bank supervision, and has been established as the independent bank regulator.

A Confucian Banking Model?

China's President Xi Jinping writes of combining the "invisible hand" and the "visible hand." This is not a sleight of hand—pun intended—as this apparently paradoxical process has been at work for thirty years.

There should be no question that in 1978 in China, socialism and "markets" were considered antithetical, just as much as they are on Wall Street. Yet as part of the structural reforms and opening-up, Deng declared, "We should have banks that operate like banks." More profoundly, what was decided, after wide debate, was that the ethical and creative features of the Chinese culture and the Chinese people must be advanced.

The first post-Mao Confucian conference was organized in 1978 at Shandong University, and state support was given to the formation of the Confucian Research Institute in Qufu. The establishment of the Academy of Chinese Culture, with the inclusion of the Studies on Modern New Confucian Thought project in the seventh five-year plan for social sciences (1986-1990) followed, and continues.[4]

Fourteenth National Congress of the ruling Communist Party of China. Picture taken in October 1992.

Most Americans would be surprised to learn that in a famous speech during his 1992 tour of southern China, Deng closed a fundamental debate in China over whether the private sector was "socialist" or "capitalist." The answer, reflecting much deliberation, was that the criteria for judgment should be whether or not it was beneficial in developing the productive forces of socialist society, reinforcing the national strength of the socialist country, and increasing the people's living standards: A very Confucian judgment, of which Solon would also approve. The Gordian ideological knot was cut!

This required more differentiated mechanisms to carry forward national banking and credit. Commercial lending was therefore separated from the PBC and moved into four "specialized banks," with the idea of providing directed credits more widely and effectively. These are now commonly referred to as China's "Big Four" banks. Several other commercial lending banks were also set up, including a reorganized Bank for Communications, CITIC Industrial Bank, and Everbright Bank.

Deng Xiaoping and his collaborators and policy planners had determined that producers must be supported and given incentives, and therefore they boldly acted, despite resistance. They began in agriculture, permitting private plots, and went on to encourage family businesses and the bazaar trade, and enabled them to hire labor. These policies, with wide discussion and debate, were spread across China's economic sectors. This was critical for a country with agricultural crises and food shortages. Again, the lesson applied was from Confucius: "The highest knowledge is that reality is impacted; Only when it engages has reality reached its height. Then ideas become true, only then is the consciousness just."

By 2004, China's State Development Planning Commission was finding that the private sector potential, which now accounted for fifty percent of the nation's GDP, was receiving only 30% of bank loans; local and regional banks were resisting private lending. In February 2005, the State Council issued several guidances, in effect relaxing fiscal, tax, and financial market access restrictions on the non-public sector. By 2005, over sixty percent of the total fixed asset investment was private investment, including foreign investment at 15-16%.[5]

A national banking policy was being advanced, with state regulations calibrated—and reformed as necessary—to deepen structural reform.

---

4. See *Confucius: And the World He Created*, by Michael Schuman (2015) and *The Reconstruction of National Identity in Post-Mao China*, by Filippo Mauri, 9/30/2008.

5. *Chinese Private Sector Development in the Past 30 Years: Retrospect and Prospect*, Hongliang Zheng and Yang Yang, March 2009, China Policy Institute, Discussion Paper 45, University of Nottingham, United Kingdom.

China's Policy on Banks and Glass-Steagall

The 14th National Congress of the Communist Party of China (1992) announced that the objective of the Chinese economic system reform was to establish a "socialist market economy." However, in the early 1990s, some financial institutions began treating the inter-bank lending market as an easy and low-cost place to raise funds to invest in real estate. They also "speculated with savings deposits in the stock market. By the summer of 1993, deposits in commercial banks were insufficient to cover development needs." New solutions were required. The commercial banks would have their role, but would no longer be left to set *de facto* policies.

The result was that the State Council determined that the PBC would be given power to independently conduct the monetary policy of the nation. The PBC, in turn, issued in June 1993, *Some Opinions Regarding the Current Economic Situation*. In that document, it announced that the PBC would "separate commercial banks from their affiliated trust and investment firms. ..." Further, in a concise document consisting of ten bullet points, the "Memorandum of the CPC Central Committee, 14 November 1993," defined the PBC's new power, under the State Council, to "conduct monetary policy independently," and "supervise all other financial institutions," and further stated, "The banking business and the securities business shall be separated." A number of Chinese specialists report that these measures were modeled on the U.S. Glass-Steagall law of the time, or otherwise state that the measures were equivalent to Glass-Steagall.[6]

This is the context in which the three new policy banks were created, independent of the PBC and directly under the State Council. The three policy banks would now oversee government-directed spending and government financial operations aimed at what President Xi now calls "the realization of the Chinese Dream." These three state-owned policy banks are the Agricultural Development Bank of China (ADBC), the

Schiller Institute

The author addresses an event on the Belt and Road Initiative held at Rice University in Houston.

China Development Bank (CDB) and the Export-Import Bank of China (EXIM). The CDB specializes in infrastructure financing: It has been key in China's High Speed Rail development and much more. It was in 1998 that the central government decided to construct "a modern, comprehensive transportation system utilizing different transportation modes in a coordinated way." The result is the world's most advanced inter-modal transport system.

EXIM provides export credits, preferential loans, and more flexible payment schedules than the big commercial banks, as the world has seen in China's recent collaboration with Ethiopia and Kenya in major railroad projects. The EXIM also raises money in domestic and foreign capital markets, and originates and participates in syndicated loans.

In 2015, China's PBC recapitalized the policy banks with a total of some $80 billion in foreign exchange reserves, to support their role in the "One Belt, One Road" Initiative. A special "Leading Group for Advancing the

---

6. See "Transforming China's Traditional Banking Systems Under the New National Banking Laws" by Andrew Xuefeng Qian, in the *Georgia Journal of International and Comparative Law*, Vol. 25:478, pages 489-490; and also *Banking Reforms and Monetary Policy in the People's Republic of China*, by Yong Guo (2002). See also, "The Intrinsic Logic of China's Banking Industry Reform" by Yi Gang, in *Transforming the Chinese Economy*, Chapter 4, pages 141-143, edited by Fang Cai (2010).

Development of One Belt One Road," organized by the State Council under the direction of the Executive Vice-Premier Zhang Gaoli, oversees the Belt and Road Initiative and the policy banks' operations within it. It is precisely in this area that the potential for United States-China cooperation exists. Once the governments of China and America are agreed, an interface can be created between a U.S. National Bank and China's policy banks, in joint projects, particularly long-term infrastructure projects in the United States and third countries. This is in addition to potential U.S. collaboration with the Asian Infrastructure Investment Bank, the BRICS' New Development Bank, and the Chinese Silk Road Fund institutions. With the re-enactment of Glass-Steagall and U.S. bank reorganization at home, major U.S. banks, including a revived Export-Import Bank, could also collaborate with Chinese institutions in a major way. This is obviously something China's national leadership will have to decide in consultation with the U.S. Administration, and with their respective institutions.

The China Investment Corporation—Vehicle of Cooperation

In a speech to the Asia Financial Forum in Hong Kong on July 2, China Investment Corporation (CIC) chairman Ding Xuedong said that the CIC was open to a change in its holdings of U.S. Treasury debt, to placing those holdings into an investment in the building of new infrastructure in the United States. Ding's speech was reported in the *South China Morning Post*, Reuters, and other media. Mr. Ding's estimate of the investment needed to build a new and modern economic infrastructure in America was $8 trillion, which, he said, would not be invested by the U.S. government and private investors alone. "According to our estimate, the United States needs at least $8 trillion in infrastructure investment; there's not sufficient capital from the U.S. government or private sector. It has to rely on foreign investments." Ding commented that the CIC also wants to invest in American manufacturing capacity. What, therefore, is the CIC?

The Chinese Investment Corporation is China's sovereign wealth fund, one of the world's largest. The larger "public funds," in terms of accounting dollars-equivalent, are the Social Security Trust Fund of the United States, followed by Japan's Pension Investment Fund, and Norway's Pension Fund Global. The CIC

was created in 2007 to increase the return on investment of China's growing foreign exchange reserves. It is intent on "long term investments within the range of acceptable risks."

While ultimately reporting to the State Council of the People's Republic of China, the CIC has also been organized as an independent, profit-driven entity. It currently invests approximately $800 billion of China's $3.1 trillion in foreign exchange reserves. It was capitalized by the Chinese Finance Ministry's issuance of special treasury bonds, largely to the People's Bank of China. The PBC paid in foreign exchange. The CIC is now responsible for paying the interest on those special treasury bonds, as well as covering all of its own administrative costs. As of 2014, the CIC had been averaging an annual return of 5.66 percent since its inception in 2007.

It is relevant to mention here the role of the state-owned Central Huijin Investment Co., Ltd., founded in 2003 as an investment company. It was then absorbed into CIC in 2007, as a wholly-owned subsidiary. Ding Xuedong, formerly a deputy director of the State Council, is CEO of both CIC and of Central Huijin. The important role of Central Huijin is in influencing, directly on behalf of the State Council of the People's Republic of China, the policies of the important, domestically based "Big-Four" banks. When founded under SAFE in 2003, Central Huijin was originally sold a majority shareholder stake in each of those "Big-Four Banks" banks. Central Huijin served as the means through which the Chinese government could act—as shareholders and board members—to improve corporate governance and initiate reforms of these banks.

Although Central Huijin no longer has a majority shareholder position, it still has such a governance role for the State Council. As identified by Bloomberg, "Central Huijin Investment Ltd. operates as an investment company. The Company provides investments in state-owned bank, insurance, finance, and securities sectors. Central Huijin Investment offers investment throughout China."

China's 'Big-Four' Commercial Banks

Following the disasters of the "Cultural Revolution" (1966-1976), China's "Big-Four" banks were created and capitalized under China's 1978 laws, utilizing resources of the PBC. In the follow-on reforms of 1995, under the new Commercial Bank Law, these originally

People's Bank of China headquarters in Beijing.

state-owned banks were made commercial banks, to attract foreign investment and subject the banks to broader public review. The Big-Four banks are now four of the five largest commercial banks in the world. The fourth largest is HSBC.

The 1995 transformation of the "Big-Four" into full-fledged commercial banks was a further response to the chronic under-capitalization of these banks and their failure to meet the urgent requirements of financing a rapidly growing Chinese economy. Indeed, the banks were recapitalized on several occasions from 1998 through at least 2004, using the new Central Huijin Investment Ltd. in 2004. Bad assets were stripped out and transferred to asset management companies. Most non-performing loans were transferred at face value to further strengthen the banks' balance sheets. "Suck it up and move on." By 2010, all of the "Big-Four" were listed as public companies. They are:

• The Industrial and Commercial Bank of China (ICBC), originally focussed on urban areas and manufacturing. It is now the world's largest bank and public company, with more than $3.5 trillion in assets—larger than the entire British economy, as CNN phrased it. As with the other "Big-Four," it is a multinational bank, with branches around the world. It is now involved in every kind of banking activity, and has over 450,000 employees.

• China Construction Bank (CCB), focussed origi-

nally on medium and long-term infrastructure and housing projects. Now the second largest bank in the world, with 13,000 branches, it also engages, as a commercial bank, in all kinds of banking activities.

• Agricultural Bank of China (ABC), originally specializing in agriculture and rural communities and businesses. It now has 24,000 branches and 320 million retail customers.

• Bank of China (BOC), originally specializing in trade finance and foreign exchange transactions. Now the fifth largest bank in the world. It is described as the most globally active of China's banks, with branches on every continent.

As this process has unfolded, a plethora of western media and financial forces has attempted to exploit any dangers which might surface. Scare stories of "high risk" in the Chinese banking system have become daily fodder in the western press. In the third week of June, 2017, the China Banking Regulatory Commission reportedly made a request for specific domestic banks to provide information on overseas loans to domestic (i.e. China-based) companies. Bloomberg, the Dow Jones wire, and other media outlets went big with the story, and the Dow wire claimed that the investigation involved alleged "high-flying private conglomerates, known for flamboyant owners, political connections and acquisitive appetites." Firms mentioned were Anbang Insurance Group, Shanghai Fosun Pharmaceutical Group, HNA Group, the Dalian Wanda Group and other large, closely held conglomerates. Stocks plunged and lawsuits were threatened. What must be said, however, is that CBRC actually *did* intervene against perceived irregularities—and it should also be emphasized that China's bank regulators and legal system are fully empowered to send predators to jail.

There are, of course, further regional and local bank players in China's financial landscape, and China's policy makers and planners are continuing to experiment. In late 2016, the PBC introduced "Foreign Country Sponsored State Banks." They can do retail commercial operations in joint ventures with the PBC. A few countries, including Egypt, have become involved. City Commercial Banks began in 1995, largely as an outgrowth of urban credit cooperatives. These banks, in conjunction with local governments, can very effectively piggy-back China's big infrastructure projects like high-speed rail, as new corridors of development emerge at the level of local and regional economies, thus playing an important role. All on board.

A New Paradigm

A new global "Four Powers" arrangement is on the horizon, bring together the great nations of the United States, China, India and Russia. This has been the intent of statesman and physical economist Lyndon LaRouche. It is time that we now join together in leaving the filth of British monetarism behind. Let us conclude by quoting China's President Xi Jinping, from his 2014 "Speech at the Opening Ceremony of the International Conference in Commemoration of the 2,565th Anniversary of Confucius' Birth and the Fifth Congress of the International Confucian Association":

> …The Chinese nation has always been peace-loving. Our love for peace is also deeply rooted in Confucianism. Since ancient times, Chinese people have held in esteem ideas preaching peace:
> - "Co-ordinate and seek harmony with all nations,"
> - "Associating with the benevolent and befriending neighbors is a precious virtue of the state,"
> - "Within the four seas, all men are brothers,"
> - "A far-off relative is not as helpful as a near neighbor,"
> - "Neighbors wish each other well, just as loved ones do to each other,"
> - "A warlike state dies inevitably, no matter how big it is."
>
> The love for peace has been embedded firmly in the spiritual world of the Chinese nation, and remains China's basic idea in handling international relations.
>
> From the Opium War in 1840 to the founding of the People's Republic in 1949, the Chi-

Flickr/Foreign and Commonwealth Office
Chinese President Xi Jinping

nese nation had suffered foreign aggressions and domestic turmoil rarely seen in human history; the Chinese people had endured unprecedented tribulation. We were once on the brink of national subjugation and genocide. In the Chinese War of Resistance against Japanese Aggression alone, our nation paid a heavy price of thirty-five million deaths and injuries. Having been through the long-term miseries in modern history, the Chinese people have the keenest understanding of the value of peace and the importance of development. The Chinese people are deeply aware that peace is essential to humanity, just like air and sunshine. Without air and sunshine, things cannot survive and grow.

> Don't do unto others what you don't want others do unto you. China needs peace, loves peace, is also willing to do its utmost in preserving world peace, and to sincerely help people haunted by war and poverty. China will resolutely follow its path of peaceful development, and hopes all countries in the world commit to such a path and implement the idea of peaceful development in our respective policies and actions….[7]

---

7. http://library.chinausfocus.com/article-1534.html

The New Name for Peace Is Economic Development

by Helga Zepp-LaRouche

July 7—This is an edited transcript of Helga Zepp-LaRouche's keynote address to the Food for Peace Conference in New York City today.

Dear conference participants, I feel very honored to address you, even if it is by video, because I think we are all aware that we are involved in the historically, extremely important process of trying to improve the relationship between the United States and China, in the context of the Belt and Road Initiative.

It is especially important in the area of agriculture and food production, because this is an extremely urgent question. Because, while at the G-20 meeting in Hangzhou last year, China and all the other participating nations devoted themselves to eradicate poverty by the year 2020, we have not yet reached that goal. Just a couple of days ago, the UN Food and Agriculture Organization put out a report that world hunger is on the rise, and that the situation, especially in Yemen, is terrible. Half or more of the population is in acute danger of starvation. But also in Nigeria and South Sudan and many other areas, the situation is worsening.

Today, there is also the G-20 summit in Hamburg, and the outcome will be a surprise, either way, because compared to last year's G-20 in Hangzhou—which was very harmonious and characterized by a great optimism for the future of mankind—this time the tensions are very high. In the last couple of days, however, there has been a sort of prelude in the form of a summit between President Putin and President Xi Jinping, in Moscow, which was really extremely important, and each characterized it as the most important event of the year for his nation. They deepened the strategic partnership, they established an even deeper level in their personal friend-

Schiller Institute

Helga Zepp-LaRouche

ship, and they declared that the time of the unipolar world is over, because of the strategic partnership, especially.

It is certainly true that the time of the unipolar world is over, but multipolarity is still not the solution, because it still implies geopolitics, which was the cause of two world wars in the 20th Century, and this geopolitics is still in operation, around North Korea, around Syria, around Ukraine.

We must therefore find a higher level. We must get the world to what President Xi Jinping always calls "the community for a shared future of humanity." One big step in that direction could be the meeting between President Trump and President Putin, who are meeting today for the first time as presidents. Obviously, this is a very important step, because a very positive relationship has already been established between President Trump and President Xi Jinping already. So whatever comes out of this Trump-Putin meeting is very, very crucial, because the questions we have to solve are urgent and dramatic.

The Many-Sided Crisis

The food crisis, the hunger crisis which I mentioned, is only a symptom of the fact that the old economic model is not functioning any more. We are sitting on a powder-keg crisis which erupted in 2008, which could come back with a vengeance—only much, much worse. Because even a slight increase in the interest rate, moving away from quantitative easing, could lead to a blowout of corporate debt. The firms which got the zero-interest-rate liquidity from the central banks, the quantitative easing, did not use this money for productive investment, but for so-called financial engineering, by buying up their own stocks to make their books look better, having more nominal value, but also increasing the corporate debt, which could now blow out if there is an increase in the interest rate.

And that is only one aspect of the systemic crisis that we still have. Another one is the so-called Level 3 derivatives that many European and other banks are sitting on. Level 3 derivatives are those that have no market price because no one will buy them, and the banks still keep them as assets, which really is a sort of mega-fraud.

So the problem is that just yesterday, the fourth largest bank in Italy was taken over by the government, and the take-over was combined with a bail-in, whereby the customers could only sell their bonds and stocks at 18 cents to the euro, and that is a threat that is hanging over the entire banking system.

Now, what could be done to solve this? Well, let's look at one other aspect of the crisis: Just a couple of days ago, in one single day, 12,000 refugees arrived from Libya in little boats and were picked up by NGOs in Italy. Twelve thousand people in one day overstretches the capacity of any country, and Italy has already taken in so many million people. But when Italy requested that other countries on the Mediterranean, such as Spain and France, should take some of the refugees, these countries rejected the proposal.

Now that obviously shows there is no unity in the European Union on this question.

The One Solution

Now how could you address this whole series of problems? What should actually be on the agenda of the G-20 in Hamburg?

Well, if you were to put a global Glass-Steagall bank separation on the agenda, doing exactly what Franklin D. Roosevelt did in 1933—by separating the commercial banks and the investment banks, putting the commercial banks under state protection, writing off the non-performing debts and the derivatives of the investment banks, and then going to a Hamiltonian credit system by setting up national banks in every country and issuing large-scale, low-interest rate credits—then we could solve the problem.

Mr. LaRouche has defined Four Laws to remedy the financial crisis, and the Fourth Law is a crash program for the realization of thermonuclear fusion power. And there the good news is that China has just accomplished a major breakthrough in this respect, with its tokamak in Hefei [the Experimental Advanced Superconducting Tokamak (EAST)], which reached what is called "steady-state H-mode operation" for 101.2 seconds. This is a major step towards the realization of thermonuclear fusion.

If such a reorganization according to these Four Laws—Glass-Steagall, national bank, credit system, and crash program for fusion and space technology—were implemented, then the trans-Atlantic countries could cooperate with such banks as the Asian Infrastructure Investment Bank (AIIB), the New Development Bank, and others, together with China, and build up, for example, Africa. China is so far the only country which has done something to fight the root causes of the refugee crisis, by investing on a large scale in rail lines in Africa, in dams, in power plants, in industrial parks, and in agriculture. And this is actually the only way to solve the refugee crisis in a human way.

China and the U.S. Can Make It Happen

One promising step in this right direction is that President Xi Jinping and Chancellor Merkel agreed yesterday to collaborate in building the planned hydropower complex in Angola, and stated that that could be a model for cooperation between China and Germany in Africa in general.

Because of what China has been doing, in building up huge industrial complexes for the first time in Africa, Africans have a new sense of self-confidence, and they are telling the Europeans, "We don't want your sermons on good governance, we want to have investments in infrastructure, in manufacturing, in agriculture, as equal business partners."

Can we expect the G-20 to do this, to go in this direction of a global reorganization of the financial system, and then go for a real intervention in the development of Africa? Well, I'm afraid they will not.

But this will remain the task that has to be accomplished. The Four Laws of Lyndon LaRouche, and getting the United States and European countries to cooperate with China in the Belt and Road Initiative—in the New Silk Road—is indeed the approach by which you can tackle all problems in the world. But this conference, this Food for Peace conference is a very important step in that direction. As a matter of fact, to get the United States and China to work together on the New Silk Road perspective, in the New Silk Road spirit, is in my view the most important aspect of this process: Because if the two largest economies can work together, I think we are on the right path to win for all of civilization.

Therefore, let's work together to join the Chinese dream, and to revive the American dream, because the American dream needs to be revived—it has almost been forgotten. But together, we can accomplish the dream for all of humanity.

Food for Peace & Thought— China-U.S. Agricultural Cooperation

by Marcia Merry Baker and Dennis Speed

July 10—On July 7, in Manhattan, a conference titled, "Food for Peace & Thought—China-U.S. Agricultural Cooperation," brought together an audience of some two hundred people, to hear twelve presentations on agriculture and economic science, with a focus on supporting collaboration between China and the United States, for a "win-win" drive internationally, to once and for all end poverty and hunger anywhere in the world, and lift up life for all peoples. Participants included a powerful delegation of agriculture experts from China, diplomats from the United Nations missions community, a contingent from the U.S. Midwest Farmbelt, infrastructure experts, and a very diverse audience from Metropolitan New York and surrounding states.

The co-sponsors of the day-long event were the

Jason Ross

The 12 speakers of the Food for Peace & Thought conference. Moderator Dennis Speed, on the right.

Schiller Institute, the China Energy Fund Committee, and The Foundation for the Revival of Classical Culture. The speakers on the two panels: "China-U.S. Agricultural Cooperation," and "Ending Poverty and Starting International Scientific Collaboration," are listed in a box accompanying this article. A video of the two-panel conference is now posted on the Schiller Institute site. Transcripts and reports on the proceedings are in preparation.

The occurrence of the event is highly significant because it comes in the context of an extreme emergency need for food right now in Yemen, Syria, and parts of Africa, emergencies which are being created by the geopolitics and monetarism of the expiring neo-colonialist British policy. But at the same time, we have the ever-growing benefits of the economic development impact of the Belt-and-Road Initiative, whose first world summit was in May in Beijing. Additionally, there are specific, positive potentials in the commitment to developing enhanced cooperation between the world's two largest food producers—China and the United States—as shown when their leaders, Xi Jinping and Donald Trump, met in Florida in April.

These potentials were explicitly referenced in the presentation by Wei Zhenglin, the Agriculture Attache of the Chinese Embassy in Washington, D.C. In terms of U.S. relations, Wei pointed out that U.S. Secretary of Agriculture Sonny Perdue was just in Shanghai and Beijing a week ago, celebrating the new U.S. beef shipments to China, which have come about during the

---

Food for Peace & Thought: China-U.S. Agricultural Cooperation

This July 7, 2017 forum in New York City was sponsored by The Schiller Institute, the China Energy Fund Committee, and The Foundation for the Revival of Classical Culture. The speakers at the forum for the two panels are listed below:

PANEL I
Food for Peace: China-U.S. Agricultural Cooperation

Dennis Speed, Moderator Northeast Coordinator, Schiller Institute

DeWayne Hopkins, Former Mayor of Muscatine, Iowa

Dr. Patrick Ho Deputy Chairman and Secretary General, China Energy Fund Committee, Hong Kong, China

Helga Zepp-LaRouche, Founder of the Schiller Institutes and Chairwoman of the German Schiller Institute

Lan Huasheng, Chairman of the Board of the Shenzhen Dasheng Agriculture Group

Prof. Carl Pray, Distinguished Professor, School for Environmental and Biological Sciences, Rutgers University

Wei Zhenglin, Agricultural Attache, Embassy of the People's Republic of China in the United States

Robert L. Baker, Founding member, the Schiller Institute Food for Peace; Agricultural Specialist, *EIR* magazine

PANEL II
Ending Poverty & Building International Scientific Collaboration

Mei Fangquan, Professor at the Agricultural Information Institute, Chief Expert of the UN Global Food Security Committee, China

Prof. Beverly Silver, Chairman of the Department of Sociology and Director of the Arrighi Center for Global Studies at the Johns Hopkins University

Wen Tiejun, Executive Dean, Professor, College of Agriculture and Rural Development, Renmin University, China

Dr. Hal B.H. Cooper, Jr. Chairman, Seattle Freight Transportation Advisory Board; expert on the Bering Strait railroad tunnel

Zhou Yingheng, Professor at Nanjing Agricultural University, China

Benjamin Deniston, Researcher, *21st Century Science & Technology* magazine; co-author, *The New Silk Road Becomes the World Land-Bridge*

DeWayne Hopkins, former Mayor of Muscatine, Iowa.

Wei Zhenglin, Agriculture Attache, Embassy of China in the United States.

Feifei Yang playing the erhu.

Visiting Shenandoah Farm, in Duchess County, N.Y., hosted by brothers Verne and Wayne Jackson, whose family has owned it since 1892. It is now part of the 10-farm dairy cooperative, which markets "Hudson Valley Fresh" products.

"100-day" period of new China-U.S. economic relations, mandated at the Xi-Trump Mar-a-Lago April meeting. In contrast, Wei reported frankly that in the recent past, U.S.-China relations were strained. Chinese agriculture technological exchange groups were treated by the U.S. Department of Agriculture as simply tourists.

The tenor of the July 7 Food for Peace conference was entirely different. The welcome to the event was given by DeWayne Hopkins, former Mayor of Muscatine, Iowa (2012-2015), on the Mississippi River. Hopkins pointed out that he comes from the heartland of the Farmbelt, where he had personally welcomed Xi Jinping, then China's Vice-President, in 2012, for Xi's return visit to Muscatine, where Xi had first stayed in 1985 while on an agriculture tour. Since then, there have developed many Muscatine connections to China. Iowa's former governor, Terry Branstad, is now the U.S. Ambassador to China, and is a personal friend of Xi. Hopkins called for everyone all over the world to treat each other in the spirit of "neighbors."

In keeping with this spirit, Classical musical selections opened both conference panels. The first piece was a string duo, "Music in the Air," featuring the Chinese *erhu* and 'cello, playing "Horse Race" and "Kang Ding Love Story." The second panel was opened by the Schiller Institute Chorus, presenting the spiritual, "Deep River," and the Civil War song, "Rally 'Round the Flag, Boys."

The intent of the Food for Peace conference especially included fostering people-to-people contact among the high-level Chinese guests and U.S. farmers, as well as Americans generally. On July 8, some twenty-five Chinese agriculture specialists were joined by nine U.S.

farm representatives, to visit a dairy farm in the Hudson River Valley. En route on their bus, the farmers and Chinese guests conferred on actual farming conditions in China and North America, finding much to their surprise on both sides.

Following the dairy farm visit, the entourage, joined by others from the July 7 audience and friends, met at Hyde Park to tour the home (and farm), library and grave-site of President Franklin Delano Roosevelt and his wife, Eleanor. Gathering at the Henry Wallace Center, named for FDR's two-term Agriculture Secretary and Vice President, the group received a briefing from Bob Baker, one of the July 7 speakers and Farm-belt liaison for the Schiller Institute, on Henry Wallace (and his father and grandfather before him), and their contributions to American System agriculture and science.

Robert L. Baker

Touring the home of Franklin Delano Roosevelt, at Hyde Park, on the Hudson River in New York. There were tours also to the FDR Presidential Library & Museum and the Henry A. Wallace Visitor and Education Center.

U.S. farm delegations came from South Dakota (four people), Minnesota (two), and two from Iowa. There were messages of greeting from James Benham, President of the Indiana Farmers Union, and from the Kansas Cattlemen's Association.

Timing of the Conference: 'Agenda 2030'

The timing of the July 7-8 Food for Peace activities was also highly significant. Many of the Chinese speakers and participants at that forum are part of China's delegation to a special U.N. event July 10-19, "High Level Political Forum on Sustainable Development," which theme is, "Eradicating Poverty and Promoting Prosperity in a Changing World." There will be many NGO side-sessions. The last two days of the forum will have ministerial-level participation and will issue a declaration. The forum will be chaired by the ambassadors to the UN from Austria and Jamaica. Some fifty nations have submitted papers in advance.

On July 6 at the United Nations, many of the same Chinese agriculture speakers who would address the Food for Peace July 7 conference, also spoke at the NGO event, "Agriculture for Sustainable Development," which was co-sponsored by the China Energy Fund Committee, the U.N. Department of Economic and Social Affairs (DESA), and the Shenzhen Dasheng Agriculture Group. Its theme was to address the fact there are about 795 million people undernourished worldwide.

"Eradicating hunger" is "Number 2" of the current round of "Sustainable Development Goals," intended to succeed by 2030. The "Number 2" goal calls on the international community to "End hunger, achieve food security and improved nutrition, and promote sustainable agriculture by 2030."

In 2015, the UN General Assembly launched this effort, calling it the "Agenda 2030" project. The other sixteen goals on the list include safe water, sufficient power, health care and so on. Needless to say, past rounds of U.N. development goals came and went unfulfilled, because, until now, no alternative emerged to successfully displace the collapsing monetarist system, which system—the neo-colonialist City of London/Wall Street system of "free" (rigged) trade, speculation, and looting, caused the impoverishment in the first place. China's Belt and Road Initiative (BRI) has changed all that.

China has intervened in UN institutions for this BRI positive-growth perspective in critical ways over the past eighteen months. To begin with, China was the first nation to issue a blueprint to the United Nations, after the 2015 General Assembly vote for the 2030 Project, to outline how poverty can truly be eradicated worldwide: The BRI is key. In March, 2016, the Belt and Road perspective was associated with the U.N. World Food Program. In September 2016, a Memorandum of Understanding (MOU) was struck between China and the U.N. Development Program, endorsing the BRI. The MOU was drafted by China's National Development and Reform Commission, which implemented China's anti-poverty success: raising 700 million Chinese out of poverty over the past thirty years. The UN General Assembly voted to combat poverty through backing for the BRI, in an action taken earlier this year.

This rapidly-spreading BRI impact for development is the realization of the inspiration and efforts going back decades, by Lyndon LaRouche and Helga Zepp-LaRouche.

Many conference speakers, while talking about crops, seeds, livestock, farming practices, and food, referred specifically to the Belt and Road Initiative, or to the LaRouches' work. Prof. Carl Pray of Rutgers University, for example, addressed the great potential in crop genetics achievements that he sees possible through new collaboration between the U.S. and China, which he called "agriculture along the New Silk Road."

It is not possible here, to summarize each of the twelve panelists' presentations, but we highlight three areas of concepts:

1) economic science,

Ho C. P., Patrick, Deputy Chairman and Secretary General of the China Energy Fund Committee.

2) the success of China in agriculture and rural development, and

3) proposals and advisories.

Potential Relative Population Density

The idea that there are insurmountable limits to resources for expanding agriculture and food, and that population must be suppressed, was roundly denounced. Dr. Patrick Ho C.P., Deputy Chairman and Secretary General of the China Energy Fund Committee, led off his presentation by denouncing Malthus in particular, and also denouncing the 20th century version of this bunk, in the Club of Rome's *Limits to Growth* book. Ho went on to describe aspects of expanding agriculture to meet a growing population.

Benjamin Deniston, Researcher, 21st Century Science & Technology magazine, led off his remarks by

Benjamin Deniston, co-author, The New Silk Road Becomes the World Land-Bridge.

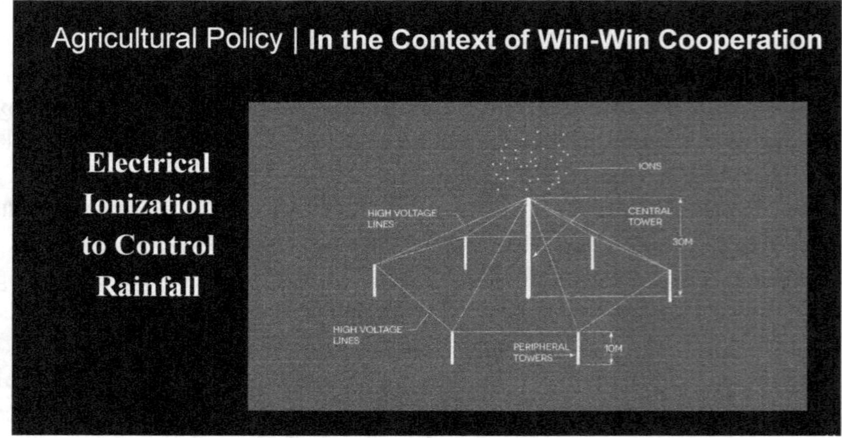

The schematic shown here, of ionization arrays to induce rainfall, has been successfully tested in Mexico, Australia, the U.A.E., Israel and elsewhere, and now is under R&D in China.

presenting Lyndon LaRouche's refutation of "Limits to Growth," in terms of the ability of the human species to exert creativity and intervene to deliberately create "new" natural resources, and thereby constantly increase the potential relative population density of humankind. One example of this kind of intervention, is to understand and expand usable water resources. Deniston gave a short update on the progress in inducing rainfall through ionization methods, and explained the significance of understanding the phenomenon of "atmospheric rivers," of potentially tapping into these water vapor configurations of Earth.

Bob Baker, a founding member of the 1988 Schiller Institute Food for Peace Initiative, gave an illustrated presentation, for crop farming, of LaRouche's breakthrough concept of "energy flux density"—the metric for measuring economic progress in terms of increasingly powerful and concentrated applications of energy. Baker pointed to increased energy flux density as shown historically in successive advances in technology for three farm field crop functions: tillage, planting, and harvesting.

China Provides 'Universal Lessons'

Most significant to everyone at the conference, was the outstanding fact of China's advancement of agriculture over the past forty years, and the lifting of 700 million people out of poverty at the same time. Many Chinese experts presented exciting aspects of this. The implications of the process for what can and must be done in Africa, in reconstruction in Southwest Asia, in the Mediterranean Basin and in all points of need, were dramatically clear for all to see. A summary of the story of Chi-

na's great success, in this short report is the presentation given by Mei Fangquan, both at the July 6 United Nations event and on July 7 at the Food for Peace conference. He has been engaged in scientific research at the Chinese Academy of Agricultural Sciences (CAAS), focusing on grain and food security and China's agricultural development strategy.

Mei's presentation was titled, "Universal Lessons from China's Advancement in Agriculture." Mei outlined three major structural phase-changes in China over the past several decades.

First, as of 1984, the nation of China had achieved the condition of a reliable food supply, with a surplus of grains. This allowed the consideration of a shift in some of the grain capacity, for certain chosen purposes. For example, some land area could be switched to cotton

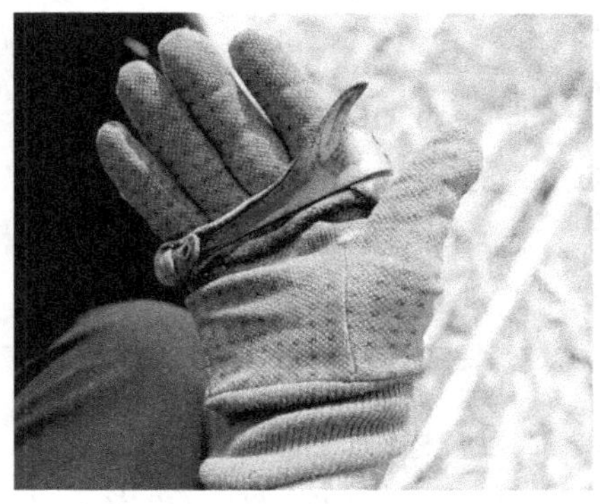

An old handheld device to aid picking a single ear of corn off the stalk.

Robert L. "Bob" Baker, 1988 founding member of the Schiller Institute Food for Peace initiative; EIR magazine, agriculture specialist.

A John Deere grain combine-harvester, with a 16 row corn head.

production. Plus, the decision could be made to use more of the grain output for livestock. This was done.

China's agriculture went from a situation in 1980, in which eight percent of the grain capacity went for feed grain for livestock, to the situation in 2010, in which 38% of total grain is feed grain for livestock. The goal by 2030, is for 50% of grain capacity to be livestock feed grain.

This shift is reflected in the improvement of the quality of food consumption. For example, the kilograms in the average diet per year, from 1995 to 2020, went down for grain foods, from 232 to 173, while they went up for meat, eggs, fish, dairy, and fruit.

Now, in addition to this process of dietary improvement, Mei said that a new process of ecological improvement is underway, in which agriculture is maintained and adjusted, while at the same time there is re-forestation, land restoration, and related upgrades. For example, a report was given on a national project to use salt-tolerant oats, not only to get a better oats crop, but for the beneficial effect it has over time to reduce salination in the soil.

This became one of the topics of exchange during the 'bus dialogue,' when Minnesota farmer Andrew Olson asked about "where the salt went" from the oats effect, and Dr. Ren Changzhong, Director of the National Oat Improvement Center (and editor of *China Oat* and *China Buckwheat*), gave a fascinating reply, ranging from which variety of oats is effective, to how many years the cultivation has to go on to benefit the soil.

MERCI: Reconstruction for MENA

Dr. Ho introduced a special proposal—called "MERCI"—in his presentations on July 6 at the U.N., and at the Food for Peace conference. It stands for the "Middle East Reconstruction Initiative." He spoke of the need for reconstruction all across MENA (the Middle East North Africa), and that we should make

By the years 2030, 50% of the total grain demands will be used as animal feeds.	
Proportion of feed grain in total grain	
1980	**8%**
1990	**21%**
2000	**33%**
2010	**38%**
2020	**43%**
2030	50%

The steadily increasing amount of grain going for livestock feed, 1980 to the present, in China.

Jason Ross

Mei Fangquan, Professor, Agricultural Information Institute; Chief Expert of the UN Global Food Security Committee, China.

Development analysis on major foods consumption in China 中国主要食物消费的发展分析								
Year	Country	Grains	Meats	Eggs	Aquatic	Milks	Fruits	Vegetables
1995	**China**	**232**	**29**	**11**	**11**	**4**	**32**	**144**
2000	**China**	**206**	**25**	**12**	**12**	**7**	**35**	**139**
2010	**China**	**183**	**29**	**15**	**17**	**25**	**40**	**128**
2020	**China**	**173**	**35**	**18**	**21**	**40**	**45**	**120**
2030	China	140	35	20	24	60	50	120
1990	**Japan**	**125**	**28**	**15**	**40**	**63**	**44**	**114**

Note: unit : Kg.

The steady improvement in the Chinese diet, to include more animal protein, fish, and fruit, 1995 to the present.

agriculture the initiating goal.

Ho stated, "The MENA region, an essential pivot connecting the East and West economic circle of the Belt and Road Initiative, is an important link in China's BRI. In particular, many countries in this region are, or used to be, major agriculture countries, such as Israel, Iraq and Egypt." He said, "The purpose of MERCI is to identify ways to integrate the reconstruction of the Middle East into the framework of the Belt and Road Initiative, to discuss the role of the international community, multi-lateral development banks and the private sector in the reconstruction effort, and to draw attention to the need to reach political and economic solutions to the region's challenges. The agricultural sector is a most pertinent starting point to advance this initiative."

Every Day Counts In Today's Showdown To Save Civilization

THE PRINCIPLE OF THE FLANK:

Victory or Hell

by Lyndon H. LaRouche, Jr.

The ancient Roman army was destroyed by Hannibal through his double-flanking operation. A greatly superior force of the Austrians was defeated in their well-designed copy of Hannibal's defeat of the Roman military, a copy of which was successfully accomplished by defeat of the superior mass of Austrian forces by a lesser force directed by Frederick the Great, at Leuthen. The principle in both exemplary cases was secured not through military forces as such, but by the principle of strategies which inheres in the human mind, not the nominal strength of the troops as such. The issue in such cases, is not forces as such, but the superior principle which the mind of the commander and his forces have brought to bear. War is best won by other means.

A crucial example of this principle was demonstrated by the advice of the General Douglas MacArthur who advised President John F. Kennedy not to permit a protracted U.S. land-war in Asia; Kennedy agreed, and Kennedy was assassinated because he opposed a war which the British conceived as a means to ruin Britain's most capable rival, our United States. By means of the assassination of Kennedy, the war proceeded, and the United States has been ruined to great British satisfaction, ever since. Such matters are essentially expressions of the battles of the mind, as certain U.S. Presidents have served the British imperial intentions ever since the assassinations of President Kennedy and his brother Robert.

In a similar fashion, the United States has been ruined by aid of Presidents such as Barack Obama, whose essential loyalties have been expressed in his impassioned ties to the British imperial Queen.

The only proper issue in fighting a war, is that there is no alternative. Considering the risk, and the costs of entering a state of warfare, it were better that it never need be fought at all. If necessary, develop the capabilities needed to defeat an enemy whose predatory intentions might not be deterred by lesser means of restraint; in such matters, as chess masters have asserted, the threat is more powerful than the attack.

As Chancellor Bismarck had warned, Germany must not support the Austro-Hungarian empire in a new Balkan war, since such an Austrian attack on the weaker Balkan force would provoke a massive deployment of Russian forces against the Austro-Hungarian empire. If Germany were stupid enough not to blackmail the Austrian Kaiser into backing off from Austria's London-directed Balkan war, London need only eliminate Chancellor Bismarck from office, to insure that the British geopolitical warfare on the continent of Europe would bring about the ruin of war-soaked continental Europe. Bismarck was discharged by British Royal family hands, and World War I, and the premises for World War II, were, so to speak, "in the bag." The British monarchy's backing of the rise of Adolf Hitler in Germany, secured the virtual inevitability of World War II and of the consequences of that war.

Notably, as former Chancellor Bismarck had warned from his place of forced retirement, the then foreseeably inevitable World War I, and also the over-

"The United States has been ruined by aid of Presidents such as Barack Obama, whose essential loyalties have been expressed in his impassioned ties to the British imperial Queen," LaRouche writes. Here, the traitor President toasts the head of America's historic enemy, the British Empire.

throw of Russia's Czar, were chiefly the British reaction to the victory of the United States under President Abraham Lincoln over the British intelligence-diplomatic services' operations in launching the British-backed Civil War in the United States. There were two principal motives of the British imperial monarchy's 1890-1917 campaign to wreck the set of nations of continental Europe through a war conceived as a grand strategy in the likeness of the British victory in its orchestration of the so-called "Seven Years War." Bismarck, in his pre-World War I forced retirement, stated exactly that point.

It is essential to understand that the British empire is an empire, an empire which is not essentially premised on colonies as such, but on the ability of its diplomats, associated intelligence services, and both witting and witless British allies and accomplices to orchestrate wars fought at great expense to the regions of the world of concern at that time. In the case of the British Empire's orchestration of the first and second "World Wars," the pivotal issue was the combined effect of the establishment of the U.S. transcontinental railway system, and the echo of the same quality of intention within not only continental Europe, but the extension into Asia: hence, Britain's avowedly

"geopolitical intentions."

Essentially, that pattern has been continued, from the reign and rampage of the New Venetian Party's representative, William of Orange, in Britain, through much more than two so-called "World Wars," in the British monarchy's steering of the imminently terminal state of general economic collapse of the United States and of many other nations, a collapse which is entering its terminal phase under the direction of the current British monarchy. If not stopped now, within as short a time as weeks, or as long as a few months, the entirety of the planet will be plunged into the most monstrous orgy of death and other ruin in known history.

Thus, at the present moment, everything depends upon the immediate re-enactment of President Franklin D. Roosevelt's 1933 Glass-Steagall legislation. There is broad-based and deeply rooted desire in the United States population to have the current U.S. President, Barack Obama, tossed peremptorily out of that office, on grounds contained within the U.S. Twenty-Fifth Constitutional Amendment; the grounds is provided by clear evidence of a mental instability in this current President, which is located within the provisions of that Amendment. Obama is a repeatedly avowed agent-in-fact of an alien power, the current British monarchy.

This occurs within a presently oncoming general breakdown-crisis of the economies of the trans-Atlantic region generally. An accelerating plunge in the physical output and wealth of the U.S.A., per capita, and per square kilometer, in which the U.S. economy is profoundly bankrupt in both financial and physical terms of per-capita assets and per-square-kilometer physical incomes, has created a condition throughout the trans-Atlantic regions, including the interior of Europe, which is now at the brink of an explosive physical-economic implosion which, if permitted would be the end of trans-Atlantic civilization, a breakdown comparable in characteristics of form to what was done to Weimar Germany in 1923, this time on a trans-Atlantic scale, rather than a single nation.

The only action which could be taken to avert such a plunge into a prolonged "new dark age" of the planet, would depend upon a certain initiating action from and by the United States: the re-installation of the 1933 Glass-Steagall law, with the exact terms specified during the 1930s decade under President Franklin D. Roosevelt. If that is done, then there must be a second action: a return to the protective economic measures used for the U.S., partly in response to World War II, then, but required as purely an economic recovery action now: price and related controls to prevent an active threat of a runaway inflation. The intention would be to return the United States, and partner-nations to the traditional agro-industrial intention of the United States which was elaborated in detail by U.S. Secretary of the Treasury Alexander Hamilton: the intention which had been established as the essentially strategic implications of the U.S. Federal Constitution.

Europe, which we are compelled to assist in the same measures of relief in our own U.S. interest, would need to get out of its particular form of current mess, by adopting a credit system comparable to Glass-Steagall's intentions and effects. The proper objective of such a rebuilding of economic policy, is to establish a fixed-exchange-rate credit system among nations, with a view to facilitating globally extended cooperation in long-term, capital-intensive modes of upward leaps in physical productivity throughout the planet.

We must recognize, at the same time, history does not exist on what many identify, symbolically as a flat plane. That brings us here to the particular intention of making clear why we require a return to a system of what are, respectively, sovereign nation states.

Cows, Horses, Chickens, and Pigs

The notion of a "one world" society, means what would be, inevitably, a world empire of the worst possible quality. It would mean a world-dictatorship of an entrenched and entire form of tyranny which would be, in respect to all of its objectionable aspects, a form of imperial grip and mass-murderous proclivities, called "governance," comparable to, but probably worse than the Roman Empire at its ugliest. Today, it is chiefly the United States, China, and India, which are the chief,

still-standing ramparts from which the threat of an inherently pro-genocidal "green" tyranny is already seeking to rule the world.

To secure a practicable form of understanding of this challenge to even the merely continued existence of some degree of human standards of human life on this planet, we must examine the case for the principle of the sovereign nation-states system. That system implicitly defines a specific quality of human interest on which present efforts to defend an actually human quality of human existence now depend.

What, in brief, is the difference between the human being and the edible features of cows, pigs, chickens, and the like? The answer is: nothing but those creative powers of reason, powers which are lacking in every other form of life presently known to us. It is, in short, those noëtic powers specific to the human individual, the power to make revolutionary developments of progress in the general condition of mankind, and that universally if we choose to adopt that standard of practice.

The creative powers of reason specific to the human species, are customarily found in the Classical artistic expressions of composition, although not the prevalent standard of art practiced among populations since the 1950 European adoption of the existentialist doctrine of the Congress for Cultural Freedom. It is the development of the creative powers of the individual, and the sharing of the qualities and fruits of those specific kinds of powers, which provide the essential development of personal character of the human individual. The Classical function of metaphor in both art and the creation of the discoveries of what are truly universal physical principles defines the truly human form of biological prototype as Russian Academician V.I. Vernadsky did with the advent of his development of the concept of a Noösphere.

Our war for today, is a war of defense of the principle which separates the truly human individual from the lower forms of life. Creativity, as I have referenced that conception here, and in other published locations, is the true standard of humanity, the quality which expresses the essential distinction of man from vegetable and beast.

Therefore, defend the true nature of mankind, while we are still able to do so. The time is short, and the opportunity brief. Act now, without fear-driven capitulations to the evil which is seeking to close in upon us presently.